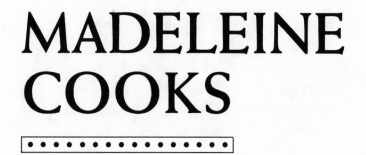

MADELEINE COOKS

Also by Madeleine Kamman

The Making of a Cook (Atheneum, 1970)
Dinner Against the Clock (Atheneum, 1973)
When French Women Cook (Atheneum, 1976)
In Madeleine's Kitchen (Atheneum, 1984)

MADELEINE COOKS

A Wonderful Teacher
Reveals the Secrets of
Cooking Great Food
Every Day
by
MADELEINE KAMMAN

Color Photography by Matthew Klein
Drawings by Richard Pfanz

WILLIAM MORROW AND COMPANY, INC. NEW YORK

Library of Congress Catalog Card Number: 85-62641

ISBN: 0-688-06203-2

Printed in the United States of America

4 5 6 7 8 9 10

BOOK DESIGN BY BETH TONDREAU

TO MY STUDENTS
ALL ACROSS AMERICA

ACKNOWLEDGMENTS

This book is a companion piece to a TV series, and together these efforts include the work of dozens and dozens of people. For the book I would first like to thank Maria Hausmann, who tested and tasted most of the recipes. I would also like to thank my 1985 students: Joanne Tenanes-Weir, Holly Berninck, Kim Horner, Augustine Alderete, and Kendra Horstmeyer, who helped in the styling of the food for the photography as well as doing recipe testing. Next, I would like to thank my editor, Maria Guarnaschelli, and Barbara Prisco, who typed the manuscript. I would also like to thank messrs. Pierre Le Vec and Pierre Moulin of Pierre Deux who generously provided the lovely plates and table linens for the pictures. I would also like to thank my neighbors in New Hampshire, particularly Richard Plush of Log Cabin Antiques.

I also want to thank the television people involved in this project: Michael B. Styer of Maryland Public Television, Sue Breger, the executive producer of the series, Joanne Kaufman of Public Television in Washington, D.C., and Charles Pinsky, the producer and director. A final thanks to Isabelle Chagnon who speaks French to me when I'm too tired to speak English.

CONTENTS

Acknowledgments   vii

CHICKEN   1

Homemade Chicken Broth   5
Chicken Cutlets with Apricots and Ginger   7
Country Chicken Cutlets with Mushrooms and Bacon   8
Chicken Cutlets with Coriander and Lime   9
Grilled Chicken Cutlets with Cranberry Compote   11
Grilled Chicken Cutlets with Red Plum Mustard   13
Pecan-Coated Chicken Cutlets with Ham   14
Breaded Chicken Cutlets with Noisette Butter   16
Broiled Chicken Etruscan-Style   18
Broiled Chicken Tunisian-Style   19
Mushroom Chicken in a Bag   21
Whole Chicken in a Bag with Zucchini and Basil   22
Roasted Chicken Legs with Mushrooms and Sherry   24
Roasted Chicken Legs with Zucchini   25
Roasted Chicken Legs with Cucumbers   26
Broiled Chicken Legs with Mustard Crumb Coating   27
Lime-and-Basil-Marinated Chicken Thighs   28
Chicken-Leg Sauté with Macadamia Nuts and Pineapple   29
Jambonettes Stuffed with Almonds and Ham   30
Dark Meat Chicken Fricassee with Dill and Lemon   33

Vegetable Accompaniments   35

Grilled Butternut Squash and Rutabaga   35
Wilted Mustard Greens and Cherry Tomatoes   36
Stir-Fried Zucchini and Hazelnuts   37
Sautéed Green Beans in Basil Butter   37
Stir-Fried Carrots and Zucchini with Dill   38
Celery, Raisins and Walnuts   39
Julienne of Celery Root   39

STEAK AND POTATOES   41

Classic Panfried Steak with Red Wine Sauce   46
Pan-Roasted Tenderloin with Red Wine Béarnaise   47
Salt-Pan Broiled Steak, Bistro-Style   49
Diet Butter   50
Michael's Grilled Steak   51
Grilled Steak with Walnut and Roquefort Butter   52
Venisoned Steak   53
Rissolé Potatoes   55
Swiss Baked Potatoes   56
Red Parsleyed Potatoes Cooked in Broth   57
Stock Potato Gratin   58
Cream Potato Gratin   59

GRAINS   61

Oatmeal and Fresh Fruit (Bierchermuesli)   65
Mixed-Grain and Vegetable Salad   66
Polenta Concia   68
Corn Grits with Okra and Squashed Tomatoes   69
Polenta with Spinach and Parmesan Cream   70
Semolina Gnocchi with Ratatouille   71
Vegetarian Risotto   74

Risotto with Radicchio 75
Barley and Mushroom Pilaf 77
Bourbon Bulgur Pilaf 78
Bulgur Cutlets 78
Warm Wehani Rice Pilaf Salad 79
Wild Rice Timbales with Two-Garlic Sauce 81

MODERN SALADS 83

Simple 87

Classic Green Salad 87
Spinach and Asparagus Salad 87
Italian Bitter-Green Salad 88
Tomato Salad with Walnut Dressing 89

Composed 91

Pear and Bacon Bits Salad 91
Greens, Fruit and Flower Salad 92
Danish Fruit and Cucumber Salad 93
Avocado, Citrus and Greens Salad 94
Provençal Rice Salad 96
Christmas Mixed-Grain and Nut Salad 97
Ham and Fruit Salad 98
Air-Dried or Smoked Meat and Melon Salad 99
Autumn Chicken and Fruit Salad 100
Warm Chicken or Duck Liver Salad 101
Smoked Turkey Salad 102
Turkey, Orange and Kiwi Salad with Tea
    and Szechuan Pepper Dressing 103
Lobster, Papaya and Avocado Salad 104
Shrimp and Green Peppercorn Salad 106
Warm Scallop Salad 107
Salmon, Asparagus and Dill Salad 108
Finnan Haddie and Potato Salad 109
Smoked Trout and Broccoli Salad 110

FISH
. . . .
111

Salmon Medallions Vapor Steamed in Plastic Wrap	114
Salmon Medallions Vapor Steamed in Lettuce Leaves	115
Salmon Medallions Mamie Soleil	117
Southern California Foil-Steamed Halibut	118
Red Snapper Fillet Escabeche	119
Chilled Ocean Perch or Snapper Fillet Escabeche	120
Mountain Trout Fillets	121
King Fish and Emperor Wine	122
Fish Fumet	123
Salt-Water-Poached Cod or Pollack Steaks	124
Poached Skate Wings with Pineapple Butter	125
Milk-Poached Finnan Haddie	127
Panfried Italian Sardines	128
Merluzzo Italiano	128
Fillet of Trout with Bacon	129
Fillet of Sole with Provençal Flavors	130
Baked Striped Bass with Sorrel Hollandaise	131
Grilled Salmon with Smoked Salmon and Bacon Butter	133
Grilled Swordfish with Gorgonzola Butter	134

SHELLFISH
. . . .
135

Stir-Fried Bay Scallops with Pistachios	138
Stir-Fried Deep-Sea Scallops with Champagne Sauce	139
Steamed Mussels Marinière	140
Steamed Mussels with Saffron and Cognac Sauce	141
Mussel Soup, Basque-Style	142
Grilled Littlenecks on the Half-Shell	143
Oysters on the Half-Shell	144
Grilled Oysters with Endive Cream	145
Olympia Oysters with Vinegared Radish	146
Small Shrimp in Danish Cucumber Sauce	147
Maine Shrimp in Their Shells	148

Shrimp and Zucchini Salad in Sun-Ripened
    Tomato Dressing   149
Steamed Lobster with Herb Butter Sauce   150
Grilled Lobster Tails with Sour Cherry Dressing   151
Sautéed Soft-Shell Crabs with Hazelnut Butter   153
Crawfish and Artichoke Hearts Etuvé   154

DUCK   157

Roast Duck American-Style with Cranberries
    and Kumquats   160
Duck Stock   162
Glazed Duck Legs with Apricot and Pistachio Couscous   163
Confit of Duck Legs with Onions and
    Strawberry Rhubarb Sauce   165
Salmis of Duck Legs   166
Broiled Duck Legs with Pear and Ginger Chutney   167
Panfried Breast of Duck with Apples and Radicchio   168
Fillets of Duck Grilled with Bitter Chocolate
    and Hazelnut Butter   169
Duck Salad   170
Duck Skin, Shallot and Breadcrumb Omelette   171

Accompaniments for Duck   172

Asparagus in Coriander Butter   172
Fiddleheads with Dried Mushrooms   173
Spaetzle   173

PIZZA AND PASTRY   175

Simple Pizza Dough (Sicilian Crust)   178
Garlic, Salt and Parsley Pizza   178
Pissaladière with Mussels and Spinach   179

Flammkuche   180

Butter Bread Dough   181

Feouse   182

Leek, Goat Cheese and Walnut Pizza   182

Pizza Dolce all'Antica   184

Panisses with Honey and Olive Oil   185

Apricot Tart   185

Zwetschkekuche   186

Rich Bacon and Ricotta Tart   188

Medieval Mushroom Tart   189

Lemon Blueberry Pie   190

Upside-down Pear Pie   192

Rhubarb Julie   193

Semi-Puff Pastry   194

Puff Pastry Shells with Snails   196

Berry Napoleon with Lemon Curd   197

Index   199

About the Author   208

INTRODUCTION

Twenty-five years ago, America became my home. Since that time, I have raised a family, run two restaurants, taught hundreds and hundreds of students, and given cooking demonstrations from Maine all the way to Alaska. What I brought with me from France was good cooking technique. What I found here was a vast store of native American products. For me, this is what defines American cuisine: a combination of fresh available ingredients with good basic cooking skills. In this book I've used that definition to create easy-to-execute recipes that reflect the modern concept for healthy eating.

There's an emphasis on the white meat of chicken, a whole range of new ideas on cooking with grains, numerous suggestions for salads that can be meals in themselves, and several unique recipes that preserve the freshness and moistness in newly caught fish and shellfish. But don't worry: I've left room for those occasional decadences. You'll find a whole chapter on steak and potatoes, one on duck that features a modern confit, and a chapter on doughs that goes all the way from pizza to puff pastry. Integrated in all these recipes are new techniques that will save you time and keep your food full of its original vitamins.

I hope this book is a useful, helpful expansion of all the recipes I've demonstrated on the television series.

Glen, New Hampshire
August 1985

CHICKEN

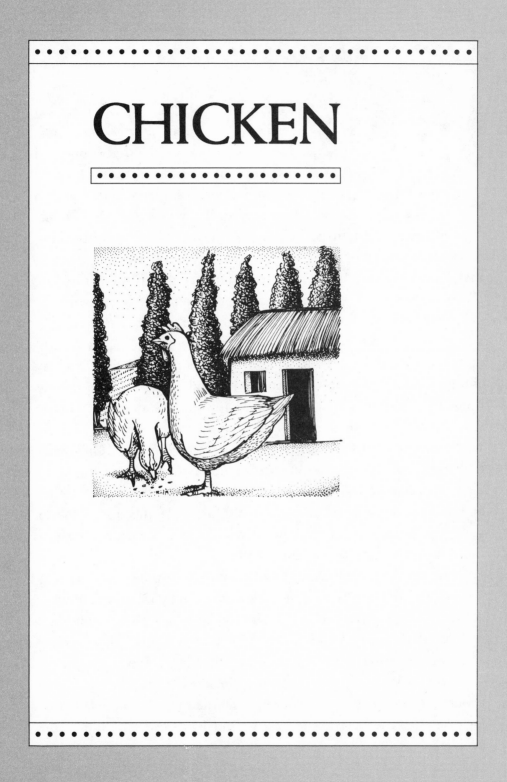

Americans love the white meat of chicken. The French, who raised me, do not, even though the practitioners of French haute cuisine in the eighteenth and nineteenth centuries made quite a fuss over it. They called the breasts *supremes* and cooked them in the blasting ovens of wood-burning stoves in a matter of minutes. But ordinary cooks like my mother, my grandmothers, and my great-aunts could afford only one chicken a week, which was roasted on Sunday. Wonderfully, I must say, but the legs were considered the choice pieces, so the white meat always ended up being somewhat overdone. As the kid of the family, I was stuck with it. It certainly was light for my child's stomach, but no one was aware that I had developed taste buds. On Sunday I had to watch Papa and Grandpapa daintily savoring the legs and thighs while I had to content myself with the white strings. Consequently, I grew up hating chicken. Only after it disappeared during World War II did I start to miss it.

After the war, chickens came back, and since only my mother and I survived, we each had a leg to enjoy. At the time, I never gave any thought to the fact that I was so casually eating some of the best-tasting chicken in the world.

I ate my first American chicken in Philadelphia on a Sunday afternoon, barbecued by my neighbor who was curious to see what a French bride looked like. She had gone to a lot of trouble and marinated the birds beforehand. The skin was marvelously crisp and tasty, but the meat had none of the flavor I was used to. I wondered, "What do they feed the chickens here?" When I read about chicken farming in America, I learned that what I was missing was the taste of grain-fed birds, and I proceeded to attack the problem.

I considered raising my own birds, discussed it with my husband and quickly realized what an impossibility that was: what about the crowing of a rooster at 5 A.M., the ruined lawn and the neighbors. Oh-la-la . . . back to the think tank, sister, you will not raise your own birds.

Well, gradually I got used to American chicken. After all, 260 million of us were consuming the same birds. I even entered the 1964 National Chicken Cooking Contest, which that year was in Easton, Maryland, and loved it. Talk about fun and a slice of Americana; I walked away with fifteen Sunbeam appliances, among them a vertical chicken roaster and an electric frying pan, which ended up being one of the great cooking discoveries of my life—believe it or not, the French have not yet invented anything like that.

I had not given up on chicken, however. About ten years later I was a judge at another chicken cooking contest, this time in Philadelphia. During a panel discussion I dared to get up and ask why chicken farmers couldn't raise free-running birds? Oh-la-la again! Frank Perdue's mouth visibly dropped, and a few women who raised chickens literally booed me. What do you mean produce a more expensive chicken? There won't be a market for it! Well, they were right: there was only a very small market for free-rangers, though now these birds are beginning to be more available.

So we have lots of chicken but we can't really say that it is wonderfully flavorful. We have to work on it to make it taste better. And as a woman who has raised a family and run two restaurants in America, I can tell you, I have worked on a lot of chickens. In that time I've found some ways to improve on taste and texture. In this chapter I'd like to share with you what I've learned. First, we consider chicken cutlets, then whole chickens, and last the legs. With the proper cooking techniques and good ingredients to give it flavor, chicken can be delicious. And remember, chicken is one of the keys to good protein without increasing calories.

COOKING CUTLETS: BONING, MAKING BROTH, COOKING TECHNIQUES

A chicken cutlet is one-half of a boneless, skinless chicken breast, often referred to as a *supreme*. What follows are several modern techniques for cooking chicken cutlets, all of which you can do on top of your stove. Here are some tips that apply to all of these techniques:

- Select two small cutlets or one large cutlet (about 4 to 5 ounces) for a single portion.
- Never use high heat when cooking cutlets or you will end up with a tough outside and an undercooked center.
- Always flatten the cutlet (approximately ½ to ⅓ inch thick)—the side of your hand is the best tool for this job.
- Whenever possible, remove the cutlet from the refrigerator 30 minutes before cooking.
- To save money, try boning your own breasts; see directions below.

Boning Chicken Breasts

Since our butchers are trying hard to modernize their work and present some meats boned and defatted, it is now easy to find boned, skinned chicken breasts in the supermarket. But it's a lot cheaper to bone your own. It's not difficult, and you can use the leftover breastbones to make your own stock. Here's a very easy and quick way to bone a double chicken breast. First, make sure you have a good chef's knife, nice and sharp; if you do not, please purchase one—you will have it in your kitchen for life. Second, have a good wooden cutting board under which you can slip a towel to prevent the board from sliding while you work.

Step 1:
Put the breast on the board with the pointed end facing you. Slide your index and middle fingers under the skin on either side of the breastbone as far as they will go.
Push forward and anchor the index and middle fingers around the

wishbone, then pull upward. The skin will lift easily. Continue pulling backward until all the white meat is exposed. Cut the skin off and discard it.

Now steps 2 and 3:

They are absolutely identical and are executed on each side of the breastbone. Turn the chicken breast so the wishbone is facing you and put the breast on its side. Cut a deep gash all along the wishbone and breastbone, hugging each of them very closely with your blade. The cut should be at least 1½ inches deep. Now turn the breast again by 90 degrees so that the cut faces you and is parallel to the edge of the board.

Holding your knife in your working hand, grasp the cutlet with your other hand so your thumb fits into the cut perpendicularly to the board. Slide your knife between the breastbone and your finger. Hold on tight to the meat and cut to the right, then to the left, hugging the bone all the time. You are now holding one cutlet. Repeat this operation on the second side to separate the second cutlet.

Now step 4:

The beautification step. You will see that there is some fat left at the edges of each cutlet. Cut it off.

The cutlet is made of a large filet topped by a small filet. On the surface of each small filet runs a small band of tendon that attaches the meat to the breastbone. Pinch that tendon at its thickest part with one hand and with your working hand slide the blade under the tendon and cut gently, going from the large end toward the thin one. The cutlet is ready.

HOMEMADE CHICKEN BROTH

Yields about 1 quart

Here is a chicken broth made with breastbones and giblets. My use of one vegetable or chicken bouillon cube gives the broth just enough salt and flavor. This broth is far less salty than the canned kind and is particularly good for deglazing since it has a lot of natural gelatin in it to thicken sauces.

Chicken breastbones, as many as you have
1 tablespoon corn oil
3 medium onions, roughly sliced
1 medium carrot, peeled and sliced
1 large leek, light green and white part only, cleaned and sliced
1 bay leaf
1 sprig fresh thyme or ½ teaspoon dried
12 parsley stems
1 vegetable or chicken bouillon cube
½ cup dry white wine (optional)
6 cups cold water
Salt and pepper

1. With a cleaver or large knife, chop the bones into small pieces. Heat the oil over moderately high heat. Add the bones and giblets and brown them well. This process will impart a lovely warm brown color to your stock. When browned, remove them with a slotted spoon and add them to a 5-quart stockpot.

2. In the same skillet, add the onions, carrot, and leek. Toss well in the pan, cover and turn heat down to low. This deglazes the pan of the chicken juices that have caramelized on the bottom. Cook the vegetables for a total of 4 to 5 minutes and then transfer them to the stockpot with the bones in it.

3. Add the bay leaf, thyme, parsley, bouillon cube, wine and water. Bring ingredients to a simmer and cook, partially covered, for an hour. Let cool and season with salt and pepper.

4. Strain through a colander placed over a mixing bowl. When the broth is completely cooled, place it in the refrigerator overnight. The next day, lift off the surface of fat that has solidified on the top.

Pan Steaming

This technique allows the cutlet to cook slowly from the outside to the center and prevents the outside from becoming overcooked. This is accomplished by using very low heat and turning the cutlet often.

CHICKEN CUTLETS WITH APRICOTS AND GINGER

Serves 6

This recipe was inspired by a visit to California, where they grow wonderful apricots.

6 large chicken cutlets, 4 ounces each
1 teaspoon powdered ginger
18 dried apricot halves (sulfur-free if possible), soaked overnight
1 teaspoon honey
Salt and pepper
2 tablespoons butter or oil
1 cup chicken broth
1 slice ginger, the size of a quarter, peeled, cut into matchsticks

1. Sprinkle cutlets with powdered ginger and let stand covered up to 1 hour to allow the ginger flavor to permeate the meat.

2. While cutlets marinate, place the apricots in a small saucepan, cover with water, bring to a boil and add honey. Lower heat and simmer until apricots are soft, about 10 to 15 minutes; puree in blender or food processor. Strain. Set aside.

3. Season the cutlets with salt and pepper. To pan steam, heat oil or butter in skillet over moderate heat. Roll the cutlets in the fat and let the meat whiten slowly on both sides. Using tongs, start turning the cutlets from side to side regularly every second minute.

4. When you touch the cutlet with the tip of your finger, you will find that it is slowly becoming stiffer. It is done when your finger does not sink into the meat anymore, between 6 and 8 minutes. Remove cutlets from the pan and keep them warm between two plates.

5. Raise the heat to high and add chicken broth. Cook until the liquid has reduced to ½ cup. Add the apricot puree and the julienne of ginger and simmer until heated through. Taste and add a pinch of salt if necessary.

6. Spoon some sauce onto the bottom of a warmed plate; place each chicken breast on the sauce and serve.

COUNTRY CHICKEN CUTLETS WITH MUSHROOMS AND BACON

Serves 6

A delicious, rich and fast dish when company's coming.

> 6 large chicken cutlets, 4 ounces each
> Salt and pepper
> 2 tablespoons butter or oil
> ½ pound fresh mushrooms, sliced
> ½ cup chicken stock
> ⅔ cup heavy cream
> 3 slices cooked bacon, crumbled
> 2 tablespoons thinly sliced scallions, green part only

1. Season cutlets with salt and pepper. Heat butter or oil in a skillet over moderate heat. Roll the cutlets in the fat and let the meat whiten slowly on both sides. Using tongs, start turning cutlets from side to side regularly every second minute.

2. When you touch the cutlet with your index finger, you will find that the meat is slowly becoming stiffer. It is done when your finger does not sink into the meat anymore, between 6 and 8 minutes. Remove cutlets from the pan and keep them warm between two plates.

3. Raise the heat and add sliced mushrooms to the skillet.

Sauté quickly until all the juices are released. Remove mushrooms with a slotted spoon.

4. Add chicken stock and let simmer for a few minutes. Then add the cream and cook until sauce coats the back of a spoon. Return cutlets and mushrooms to the pan and heat through.

5. To serve, place each cutlet on a plate and spoon sauce over it. Garnish with crumbled bacon and scallion greens.

Bag Steaming

This is a modern no-fuss way to cook chicken cutlets in plastic cooking bags which are available nowadays everywhere in supermarkets. Based on a technique that French women have used for centuries (see page 20), the chicken cutlets are placed in the cooking bag and steamed until just cooked. This technique leaves the cutlets juicy and as tender as butter.

CHICKEN CUTLETS WITH CORIANDER AND LIME

Serves 4

In this dish I've borrowed that wonderful Mexican combination of coriander and lime.

    4 chicken cutlets, about 4 ounces each
    2 tablespoons chopped coriander leaves
    ½ teaspoon lime rind, finely grated
        Salt and pepper
    1 teaspoon and 2 tablespoons oil or melted butter

GARNISH (OPTIONAL)

⅓ pound snow peas, strings removed
1 cucumber, peeled, cut in half and seeded
1 large red onion
1 tablespoon cider vinegar

1. Using the side of your hand, flatten the cutlets to between ⅓ and ½ inch thick. Sprinkle with coriander and lime rind; salt and pepper on both sides.

2. Rub the inside of a cooking bag with 1 teaspoon of corn oil or melted butter. Slide the cutlets into the bag so that they will sit flatly on the bottom of a skillet. Push all the air you can from the bag and seal it tightly.

3. Place the bag on the bottom of a large skillet and cover with a lid smaller than the skillet.

4. Pour boiling water into the skillet until the bag is covered. At this point, turn the heat onto low and allow the water to simmer for 3 minutes. Turn off heat and let stand for 5 more minutes.

5. If you want to make the garnish, while the cutlets finish steaming, cut the snow peas in half diagonally and cut the cucumber halves into ⅙-inch-thick half-moons. Slice the red onion into thin slices. In a skillet, heat 1 tablespoon of the oil or butter and stir-fry the snow peas and cucumbers for 2 minutes. In a second frying pan, stir-fry the red onion slices in the remaining tablespoon of oil or butter. After 1 minute, add the vinegar and turn off the heat.

6. When the chicken is cooked, cut open the cooking bag and place the cutlets on a serving plate. Garnish with snow peas, cucumbers and onions.

Stove-Top Grilling

The implement best adapted to this technique is a stove-top, ridged or ribbed grill. Not only does the grill give the cutlet that browned, barbecued look, it also lets you cook using very little fat. A good old-fashioned cast-iron skillet also works well.

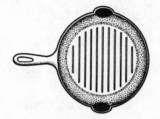

GRILLED CHICKEN CUTLETS WITH CRANBERRY COMPOTE

Serves 6

Inspired by America's rich harvest of cranberries, this is a very tasty dish.

    1 recipe Cranberry Compote (see page 12)
    6 large chicken cutlets, about 4 ounces each
    1 clove garlic, mashed
    3 tablespoons olive or corn oil
      Salt and pepper

1. Prepare cranberry compote according to the recipe on page 12.

2. Flatten the cutlets with the side of your hand to about ½ inch thick. Combine the garlic with the oil. Brush 2 tablespoons of oil over both sides of the cutlets. Cover with plastic wrap and let stand up to 1 hour.

3. Preheat the grill over medium heat. Brush the remaining tablespoon of oil on the grill.

4. Season the cutlets with salt and pepper. Grill for 3 to 4 minutes on one side or until nicely browned; turn and grill on the other side for 3 to 4 minutes, this time pushing down on the cutlets with a lid to force the meat to cook rapidly all the way to the center.

5. While the cutlets grill, reheat the cranberry compote. Serve with cranberry compote spooned around the cutlets.

CRANBERRY COMPOTE

Yields about 1½ cups

This compote is a wonderful way to use up leftover cranberry sauce.

⅓ cup dried currants or raisins
½ cup cider vinegar
1 tablespoon butter or oil
1 medium onion, finely chopped
1 clove garlic, mashed
1½ teaspoons curry powder
1½ cups tomato puree
1½ cups water
1 tablespoon brown sugar or honey, or more as needed
⅔ cup whole-berry canned cranberry sauce
1½ tablespoon Worcestershire sauce
Salt as needed, if needed
Cayenne (optional)

1. Put the currants or raisins in a small bowl. Add the vinegar and let steep for 1 to 2 hours.

2. Heat the butter or oil in a quart saucepan, add the chopped onion and garlic, and toss well until the onion is translucent. Stir in the curry; cook for 1 to 2 minutes.

3. Add the tomato puree, water, brown sugar, cranberry sauce and Worcestershire sauce, as well as the prepared vinegared currants. Bring to a boil, turn down to a simmer, and cook until a still slightly chunky mixture is obtained, or about 45 minutes. Taste and add salt if needed, more sugar if you like, or even a dash more vinegar if necessary. Depending on how hot you like your food, add as much cayenne as you see fit. The compote can be made in advance and kept in the refrigerator, covered, for several days.

GRILLED CHICKEN CUTLETS WITH RED PLUM MUSTARD

Serves 6

When plums are ripe and plentiful, make this chicken dish.

> ½ recipe Red Plum Mustard (see below)
> 6 large chicken cutlets, about 4 ounces each
> 1 clove garlic, mashed
> 3 tablespoons olive or corn oil
> Salt and pepper

1. Prepare red plum mustard according to the recipe below.

2. Flatten the cutlets with the side of your hand to about ½ inch thick. Combine the garlic with the oil. Brush 2 tablespoons of the oil over both sides of cutlets; cover with plastic wrap and let stand up to 1 hour.

3. Preheat the grill over medium heat. Brush remaining oil on the grill.

4. Season the cutlets with salt and pepper. Grill for 3 to 4 minutes on one side or until nicely browned; turn and grill on the other side for 3 to 4 minutes, this time pushing down on the cutlets with a lid to force the meat to cook rapidly all the way to the center.

5. While the cutlets grill, reheat the red plum mustard. Serve with plum sauce spooned around the cutlets.

RED PLUM MUSTARD

Yields about 3 cups

This is a summer condiment that can be made with any variety of plum you like. I suggest red ones because the color is much more attractive; wide variations in taste can be obtained if you use round plums or the elongated Italian prune plums. Try them all for fun.

　2 pounds red plums, pitted and cut into ¾-inch pieces
　½ cup dry white wine
　¼ cup honey
　1 teaspoon ginger
　⅛ teaspoon cloves
　½ teaspoon cinnamon
　¼ teaspoon allspice
　1 tablespoon cider vinegar
　　Dijon-style mustard with seeds, as needed to suit your taste
　　Salt, to taste
　　Pepper, to taste

1. Put the plums in a saucepan with the white wine, the honey, all the spices and the vinegar. Cook down to a thick sauce texture, very much like ketchup, 45 minutes or so. Puree in a blender or food processor. Strain to discard all larger traces of skins.

2. Return the plum sauce to a saucepan, reheat to warm and add as much mustard as you like. Salt and pepper to taste. Serve with the grilled chicken cutlets. The plum sauce can also be kept, covered, in the refrigerator for several weeks.

Panfrying

The only time I ever panfry or sauté a chicken cutlet is when I have first crumbed the meat. This protects the outer layer of the cutlet and keeps it from becoming tough and dried out.

PECAN-COATED CHICKEN CUTLETS WITH HAM

Serves 6

This is truly a dish made from Southern ingredients, cutlets coated with pecans and stuffed with Smithfield ham and more pecans.

6 chicken cutlets, 4 ounces each
1 tablespoon butter
6 tablespoons coarsely chopped pecans
1 large, paper-thin slice of Smithfield ham, chopped (you can also use baked or boiled ham)
Pepper

FOR THE BREADING
2 tablespoons flour for dredging
1 egg
2 tablespoons chopped parsley
1 teaspoon oil
1 teaspoon water
Salt and pepper
½ cup finely ground pecans
¼ cup breadcrumbs
2 tablespoons butter or oil

1. Place each cutlet on a cutting board, smooth side up. Cut into the cutlet halfway so that a pocket will be made. Cut at least 1½ inches deep or more if you can without separating the two sides of the cutlet.

2. Heat the butter in a skillet, add the coarsely chopped pecans and toast them lightly in the butter for 1 to 2 minutes. Stir in the Smithfield ham and add the pepper. Cool completely. Stuff each of the pockets with an equal amount of this mixture. Close the pockets by pressing the edges together.

3. Put the flour on a sheet of wax paper. In a shallow bowl, mix the egg, parsley, oil, water, salt and pepper thoroughly. In a second shallow bowl, combine the ground pecans and breadcrumbs.

4. To bread the cutlets, dredge a cutlet in the flour, then pat it well between both hands so that it retains only a thin veil of flour. Next, with a pastry brush, brush the egg mixture lightly over one side of the cutlet. Dip the egged side of the cutlet into the nuts and crumbs and let it sit while you brush the top side of the meat. Turn the cutlet over and let it sit in the nut and crumb mixture while you start the next cutlet. Place each cutlet on a cake rack to dry for at least a few minutes.

5. Heat the butter or oil in a skillet over moderate high heat. Panfry the cutlets for 2 to 3 minutes or until lightly browned. Turn them and repeat on the second side. Turn down the heat to medium and continue to cook the cutlets, turning once more until they are firm to the touch—in all, about 8 minutes.

BREADED CHICKEN CUTLETS WITH NOISETTE BUTTER

Serves 6

Here is a recipe for breaded chicken cutlets that get a sprinkling of brown butter as a final touch.

6 chicken cutlets
½ teaspoon lemon rind
3 tablespoons lemon juice

FOR THE BREADING
Juice of ½ lemon
½ teaspoon lemon rind
2 tablespoons flour
1 egg
1 teaspoon oil
1 teaspoon water
Salt and pepper
6 tablespoons breadcrumbs
2 tablespoons flour
½ cup butter, clarified, or oil

1. Blend lemon juice and rind. Brush each cutlet with a small amount of mixture. Let stand.

2. Put the 2 tablespoons of flour on a sheet of wax paper. In a small bowl, mix the egg, oil and water. Beat thoroughly with a fork. Stir in the breadcrumbs with the flour, salt and pepper.

3. Flour a cutlet, then pat it with both hands to retain only a veil of flour. Brush the egg mixture over the floured cutlet, using a

**Jambonettes Stuffed with
Almonds and Ham**

(p. 30)

**Salt-Pan Broiled
Steak, Bistro-Style**
(p. 49)

**Pan Roasted Tenderloin
with Red Wine Béarnaise**

(p. 47)

Grains,
from top left,
clockwise:
corn grits;
cornmeal;
buckwheat;
wehani,
wild and
arborio rices
(in bowl);
bulgur;
semolina;
and barley
(p. 62)

**Watermelon, cantaloupe,
honeydew and cranshaw melons**

Smoked Meat and Melon Salad
(p. 99)

Turkey, Orange and Kiwi Salad
with Tea and Szechuan Pepper Dressing
(p. 103)

pastry brush. Turn the egg-washed side of the cutlet into the bread-crumb mixture and repeat until both sides of each cutlet are floured, brushed with egg and breaded. Let cutlets sit on a rack until ready to use.

4. Heat clarified butter or oil until it bubbles. Panfry the cutlets over moderately high heat on each side until golden. Remove from pan and keep hot. Do not discard the butter or oil.

5. To the skillet add lemon juice, salt and pepper and lemon rind. Cook on high heat for a few minutes. Correct the seasoning and trickle over the center of each cutlet.

BROILING WHOLE CHICKEN

Broiling is a technique that yields the same crisp skin and juicy meat as oven roasting but in less time. Here are some tips to ensure your broiled chicken comes out tasty and with a good texture.

- Select as small a chicken as possible; 2-2½ pounds is ideal.
- Cornish hens are wonderful broiling birds.
- Always remove the backbone from the chicken so that it will lie flat in the broiling pan and therefore will broil evenly.
- Begin broiling the chicken close to the heat source to obtain a crisp skin and to seal in the juices. Then move it away to finish broiling.

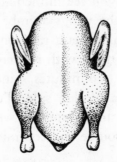

BROILED CHICKEN ETRUSCAN-STYLE

Serves 6

The combination of lemon and hot pepper brings out the flavor of the broiled chicken.

> 6 tablespoons butter, softened
> Salt
> Pepper, freshly ground
> 1 tablespoon lemon juice
> 1 tablespoon finely grated lemon rind
> ½ teaspoon red pepper flakes
> 3 broilers, 2½ pounds each or 3 Cornish hens
> Melted butter or oil for brushing broilers
> ½ cup water or chicken broth

1. Cream the butter. Add the salt, pepper, lemon juice, lemon rind and red pepper flakes to make a compound butter.

2. Insert one-third of the compound butter under the skin of each bird. To insert butter, first loosen the skin with your index finger, then slide the softened butter under the skin and flatten it evenly over the breast meat and under the leg skin.

3. To get the birds to lie flat, "frog" them. This is the best technique. Take a pair of poultry shears and cut off the backbones. Open up each bird and flatten it. Since the breastbone is somewhat rigid, push it down to break it. The breast will immediately flatten. Now push both legs upward toward the wings. Punch a small hole on either side of the tail and tuck each leg into a hole. Only after this is done, cut off the tail—you will see immediately that the bird resembles a flattened frog. Fold the wings akimbo.

4. Preheat the broiler. Set a rack on a roasting pan. Do not season the birds, but brush them with melted butter or oil. Broil the cavity side of the birds for 5 to 6 minutes, 4 inches away from the heat source; salt and pepper the broiled side. Turn the birds over and repeat on the skin side; salt and pepper. Lower the chickens to 6 to 7 inches away from the heat source and continue broiling for another 5 to 6 minutes on each side.

5. To check doneness, prick the thigh with a skewer. If the juices run clear, the bird is done.

6. Remove cooked birds to a platter. Pour off any fat that has accumulated in the pan. Add water or chicken broth to the pan and cook over medium high heat on top of the stove. Scrape to dissolve any caramelized juices. Bring to a vigorous boil and cook for a minute or two. Strain into a small sauceboat.

BROILED CHICKEN TUNISIAN-STYLE

Serves 6

The flavors of North Africa migrated with me to America.

    6 tablespoons butter, softened
      Salt
      Pepper, freshly ground
    1 tablespoon and ½ cup orange juice
    1 tablespoon finely grated orange rind
    3 broilers, 2½ pounds each, or 3 Cornish hens, halved
      Melted butter or oil for brushing chickens
    ½ teaspoon paprika
    ½ teaspoon finely minced garlic
   12 orange slices, peeled and seeded

1. Cream butter. Add salt, pepper, 1 tablespoon orange juice, orange rind, paprika and garlic to make a compound butter.

2. Insert one-third of the compound butter under the skin of each bird. To insert the butter, first loosen the skin with your index finger, then slide the softened butter under the skin and flatten it evenly over the breast meat and under the leg skin.

3. To get the birds to lie flat, "frog" them. This is the best technique. Take a pair of poultry shears and cut off the backbones. Open up each bird and flatten it. Since the breastbone is somewhat rigid, push it down to break it. The breast will immediately flatten. Now push both legs upward toward the wings. Punch a small hole on either side of the tail and tuck each leg into a hole. Only after this is done, cut off the tail—you will see immediately that the bird resembles a flattened frog. Tuck the wings under the legs.

4. Preheat the broiler. Set a rack on a roasting pan. Do not season the birds, but brush them with melted butter or oil. Broil the cavity side of the birds for 5 to 6 minutes, 4 inches away from the heat source; salt and pepper the broiled side. Turn the birds over and repeat on the skin side; salt and pepper. Lower the chickens to 6 to 7 inches away from the heat source and continue broiling for another 5 to 6 minutes on each side.

5. To check doneness, prick the thigh with a skewer. If the juices run clear, the bird is done.

6. Remove cooked chickens to a platter. Pour off any fat that has accumulated in the pan. Add the ½ cup of orange juice to the broiling pan and cook over medium heat on top of the stove. Scrape to dissolve any caramelized juices. Bring to a vigorous boil and cook for a minute or two. Add the orange slices. Spoon juices over chickens before serving and garnish with the warmed orange slices.

COOKING WHOLE CHICKEN IN A BAG

In the area of Lyon, the capital of great French cooking, women have cooked chicken in pig's bladders for centuries. This technique is still used in a few restaurants and there is no doubt that the succulence of the meat obtained is absolutely incomparable. The custom in Lyon demands that large slices of truffles be slipped under the skin of the chicken. What a treat, but what a fortune!

Millions of us, however, have survived without truffles, and, short of a pig's bladder, we now have our much appreciated plastic cooking bags, available in supermarkets, which preserve the succulence of the chicken just as well. All you have to do is put some seasonings under the skin of the chicken, place the chicken in the bag with a few vegetables and simmer it in boiling water. Perfect for low-fat diets! Perfect, too, if you like a good cream sauce because of the marvelous juices this process yields.

MUSHROOM CHICKEN IN A BAG

Serves 4 to 6

A modernization inspired by the traditional recipe of Lyon. The distinct flavor of superexpensive truffles has been replaced with the wonderful woody taste of wild mushrooms.

1 roasting chicken, 4 to 4½ pounds
  Salt and pepper
½ pound fresh mushrooms or a mixture of fresh and wild mushrooms, such as chanterelles and boleti
2 tablespoons butter or oil
¼ cup butter, softened
1 tablespoon cornstarch
1 cup half-and-half, cold
2 to 3 tablespoons chopped fresh chives or green part of scallions

1. Salt and pepper the chicken cavity.

2. Chop the mushrooms finely. Melt the 2 tablespoons of butter or oil in a skillet. Add the mushrooms, salt and pepper, and sauté over medium heat, covered, for ½ minute or until the mushrooms have given off their juices. Uncover the pan and let the juices, if any, completely evaporate. Cool completely.

3. Cream the ¼ cup of butter and stir in the cooled mushrooms.

4. Loosen the skin of the chicken completely; slide the mushroom mixture under the skin on both sides of the chicken, spreading it well over the breasts and legs. Slide the chicken into a small-size plastic cooking bag. Tie the bag tightly and seal well around the bird.

5. Bring a 5-quart pot half full of water to a boil. Add the bagged chicken so that it is immersed in boiling water. Place a lid smaller than the pot on top of the chicken to keep it immersed. Simmer for approximately 1 hour. Remove the bag from the water. Let it sit for 5 minutes. Take the chicken out and keep it warm.

6. *To make a sauce:* Strain the juices that have accumulated at the bottom of the bag and pour into a 1-quart saucepan. Bring to a boil, then turn down to a simmer. Meanwhile, mix the cornstarch with the half-and-half and stir until smooth; pour gently, stirring constantly, into the simmering juices and continue to simmer until the mixture has slightly thickened. Add the chives or scallions and correct the seasoning.

NOTE: If fresh mushrooms are not available, dried mushrooms can be substituted. To rehydrate dried mushrooms, soak in warm water for 10 minutes. Rinse well. Drain and pat dry.

WHOLE CHICKEN IN A BAG WITH ZUCCHINI AND BASIL

Serves 4 to 6

>1 roasting chicken, 4½ pounds
>Salt and pepper
>3 tablespoons butter
>1 cup freshly grated zucchini
>1 tablespoon fresh basil, chopped, or 1 teaspoon dried
>1 teaspoon fresh parsley, chopped
>¼ cup freshly grated Parmesan or Romano cheese

1. Salt and pepper the chicken cavity.
2. Melt the butter in a skillet over medium high heat. Quickly sauté the zucchini until the juices are drawn out and evaporated. Add the basil, parsley, and the cheese. Mix well.

3. Loosen the skin of the chicken completely; slide the zucchini-cheese mixture under the skin on both sides of the bird, spreading it well over the breasts and legs. Slide the chicken into a small-size plastic cooking bag. Tie the bag tightly and seal well around the bird.

4. Bring a 5-quart pot half full of water to a boil. Add the bagged chicken so that it is immersed in boiling water. Place a lid smaller than the pot on top of the chicken to keep it immersed. Simmer for approximately 1 hour. Remove the bag from the water bath.

5. *To make a sauce:* Strain the juices that have accumulated at the bottom of the bag and pour into a saucepan. Bring to a boil, and cook for a minute or two. Serve with the chicken.

Cooking in a Bag for a Crowd

Not only is this a delicious and a healthy way to cook for family and friends, it's also easy, and there is virtually no clean-up. If you wish to cook several chickens at a time, here's how:

2 roasters in a 2-gallon pot
4 roasters in a 5-gallon pot
5 roasters in a 6-gallon pot

In each case, bag the chickens separately and cook for approximately 1 hour.

CHICKEN LEGS

The chicken leg is made up of a drumstick and thigh. I prefer the thigh meat, but you can use either or both in any of the following recipes.

Tips for Roasting Chicken Legs

- A drumstick plus a thigh, two drumsticks, or two thighs make for a single, generous portion.
- Roast legs in a slow oven—325°—to develop more flavor in the meat.
- To give the legs more flavor, sprinkle with herbs and spices or slip a compound butter under the skin.

ROASTED CHICKEN LEGS WITH MUSHROOMS AND SHERRY

Serves 6

This was the meal I cooked to entertain guests when I was first married.

 6 chicken drumsticks, 6 chicken thighs
  Salt and pepper
 ¼ teaspoon freshly grated nutmeg
 1 tablespoon melted butter
 1 tablespoon raw butter
 1 pound mushrooms, sliced
 ⅓ cup top-quality dry sherry
½ to ⅔ cup heavy cream
  A few drops lemon juice

1. Preheat oven to 325°. Sprinkle chicken parts with salt, pepper and nutmeg. Brush them with melted butter and place them uncut side down on a rack in a large metal baking pan. Roast for 30 minutes, turn over and roast for another 20 to 25 minutes.

2. Meanwhile, heat the 1 tablespoon of butter in a large skillet and add the mushrooms, salt and pepper. Toss the mushrooms in the hot butter for a few seconds, turn down the heat to low and cook covered for another 1 to 2 minutes. Empty mushrooms into a strainer placed over a bowl to collect any juices.

3. When the chicken is done, remove it to a dish lined with paper towels to absorb any fat. Keep warm in a low oven. Pour off all fat in the roasting pan. Place pan on the stove on medium low heat and add reserved mushroom juices and sherry. Scrape well to loosen and dissolve chicken juices that have caramelized on the bottom of the pan.

4. Return mushrooms to skillet and strain chicken glaze over them; add the cream and cook over medium high heat until a saucelike texture results. Taste and add salt, pepper or lemon juice as you want them. Serve chicken with sauce and mushrooms spooned over the meat.

ROASTED CHICKEN LEGS WITH ZUCCHINI

Serves 6

This is a variation of the roast chicken legs with mushrooms and sherry.

    6 large chicken legs
      Salt and pepper
    1 tablespoon finely chopped parsley
    1 clove garlic, minced
    2 tablespoons melted butter
    1 tablespoon butter
    2 medium-sized zucchini, sliced thinly
    ½ cup water or broth

1. Preheat oven to 325°. Sprinkle the chicken parts with salt and pepper. Brush them with melted butter and place them uncut side down on a rack in a large metal baking pan. Roast for 30 minutes, turn over and roast for another 20 to 25 minutes.

2. Meanwhile heat the 1 tablespoon of butter in a large skillet; add the zucchini, salt and pepper. Toss the vegetables in the hot butter and turn down the heat. Continue to cook until juices are extracted and evaporated. Add parsley and garlic. Turn off heat. Set aside in skillet.

3. When chicken legs are done, remove them to a plate and keep warm. Discard all the fat in the roasting pan. Place the pan on medium low heat on top of the stove and add water or broth. Scrape well to dissolve all the brown glaze. Cook a few minutes until heated through.

4. Strain the pan juices over the zucchini. Reheat. Serve with the chicken legs.

ROASTED CHICKEN LEGS WITH CUCUMBERS

Serves 6

> 6 chicken legs
> Salt and pepper
> 2 tablespoons melted butter
> 1 tablespoon butter
> 2 cucumbers, peeled, seeded and cut in half-moons
> 2 tablespoons finely chopped mint or dill
> ¼ cup broth or water
> ½ to ⅔ cup heavy cream
> A few drops lemon juice

1. Preheat oven to 325°. Sprinkle the chicken parts with salt and pepper. Brush them with melted butter and place them uncut side down on a rack in a large metal baking pan. Roast for 30 minutes, turn over and roast for another 20 to 25 minutes.

2. Meanwhile, heat the butter in a large skillet, add the cucumber half-moons, salt and pepper. Toss in hot butter. Turn down heat. Continue to cook until juices are extracted and evaporated. Add mint or dill. Set aside.

3. When chicken legs are done, remove them to a plate and keep warm. Discard the fat in the roasting pan. Place the pan on medium low heat and add broth. Scrape well to dissolve all brown chicken glazes.

4. Strain chicken glaze over cucumbers, and add cream. Cook a few minutes until a saucelike texture results. Correct seasoning with salt and pepper and lemon juice as needed. Use as a sauce over the chicken.

Broiling Chicken Legs

The same method for broiling whole chickens applies to the legs.

BROILED CHICKEN LEGS WITH MUSTARD CRUMB COATING

Serves 6

> 6 chicken legs (thigh and drumstick)
> 4 tablespoons melted butter or oil
> ½ cup fine, fresh breadcrumbs
> Salt
> Pepper from the mill
> 1 tiny garlic clove, mashed
> 1 tablespoon finely chopped tarragon or parsley leaves
> 4 tablespoons Dijon mustard

1. Preheat the broiler. Brush the chicken legs with 2 table-spoons of the butter or oil and place them on a roasting pan fitted with a rack. Place the broiler pan 4 inches away from the flame and broil for 5 to 6 minutes on each side.

2. Meanwhile, mix well together the breadcrumbs, salt, pepper, garlic and chopped herbs. Brush the skin side of each leg with Dijon mustard and sprinkle evenly with the aromatic crumb mixture. Dribble the remaining melted butter or oil over the chicken legs and finish the broiling 6 to 8 inches away from the flames, about 6 minutes on each side or until juices run clear. Serve piping hot with Sautéed Green Beans in Basil Butter (page 37) or with Stir-Fried Carrots and Zucchini with Dill (page 38).

LIME-AND-BASIL-MARINATED CHICKEN THIGHS

Serves 6

This makes a succulent meal in the summertime when fresh basil is available.

> 1 tablespoon lime juice
> 1 teaspoon lime rind, finely grated
> Salt and pepper
> ¼ cup packed fresh basil leaves
> ¼ cup olive or corn oil
> 12 chicken thighs
> Lime slices and 6 large basil leaves to garnish

1. *To make the marinade:* Combine the lime juice, lime rind, salt and pepper, and basil leaves in a blender container. Blend until smooth, then add oil and blend until well incorporated.

2. Place the chicken thighs in a shallow dish and brush both sides of each one with marinade. Let stand for at least 30 minutes.

3. Preheat the broiler. Place the marinated thighs on a rack in a broiler pan and place pan 4 inches away from the heat source for 5 to 6 minutes. Turn, and broil for another 6 to 8 minutes.

4. Garnish each portion with lime slices and basil leaves.

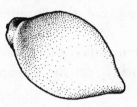

Sautéeing

This method of cooking does wonders for chicken pieces as they turn moist and delicious. This is a *"bonne femme"* cooking method, passed on to the chefs by country women.

CHICKEN-LEG SAUTÉ WITH MACADAMIA NUTS AND PINEAPPLE

Serves 6

If you cannot get fresh pineapple, certainly use canned pineapple rings, provided they are sugar-free. The expensive macadamia nuts can be replaced with slivered almonds.

> 6 chicken legs, cut into 6 drumsticks and 6 thighs
> 4 tablespoons butter or oil
> Salt
> Pepper from the mill
> ½ to 1 cup chicken broth, preferably homemade
> 1 large, fresh pineapple, peeled and cored, cut into ⅓-inch slices
> 2 tablespoons dark rum (optional)
> 18 macadamia nuts, coarsely chopped
> ¼ cup slivered scallion greens

1. Remove any excess fat from the edge of the skin covering of the chicken pieces. Heat 2 tablespoons of the butter or corn oil in a large skillet or sauteuse pan and brown the legs well. Season them with salt and pepper. Discard the browning fat, add ½ to ⅔ cup of the chicken broth, cover and cook for 20 minutes over medium heat, lid slightly askew.

2. Heat the remaining 2 tablespoons of butter or oil in another skillet. In it, quickly sear the pineapple slices on high heat so they acquire a brown, caramelized surface on both sides. Turn the heat down, add the rum and shake the pan well and let simmer for 1 minute. Cut the pineapple slices into quarters.

3. Add the pineapple pieces and any of their juices to the skillet containing the chicken and let cook together for another 10 to 15 minutes. If the juices have all evaporated, add a little more chicken broth. Correct the final seasoning with salt and pepper. Serve topped with the macadamia nuts and scallion slivers.

JAMBONETTES STUFFED WITH ALMONDS AND HAM

Serves 6

A *jambonette* means little ham. It gets this name because when the bone is removed from a leg and the meat filled with a stuffing, the result is something that looks incredibly like a little ham. For this recipe, select chicken legs (thighs and drumsticks) that are completely covered with smooth skin all in one piece.

Every one of us has had to face one of those inevitable dinner parties at a time when our pocketbook has had come to the rescue more than once. This is one of the best ways to present chicken in an elegant style with which very few people are familiar. The lack of bone to struggle with makes eating a pleasure. No difficulty in the cooking method—it is the same as I have applied above: a plain sauté. However, the boning method may be a bit of a challenge, so sit and read carefully before you start.

> 6 chicken legs, drumsticks and legs in one piece
> Salt and pepper
> ¼ cup finely diced boiled ham
> 2 tablespoons of blanched almonds, coarsely chopped
> ¼ cup fresh breadcrumbs from French, Italian or unsweetened white bread
> A pinch cayenne
> 2 tablespoons milk or light cream
> 1 tablespoon dry sherry or Madeira
> 3 tablespoons butter or corn oil
> ½ to ¾ cup chicken stock
> 1 tablespoon ground coriander
> 1 tablespoon chopped fresh coriander leaves

1. Bone the chicken legs so as to create 6 jambonettes (see boning instructions on page 32). Salt and pepper the meat on the meat side.

2. Mix together the ham, almonds, breadcrumbs, salt and cayenne to your taste, milk or cream, and sherry or Madeira until a slightly moist stuffing forms. Divide into six equal parts. Stuff each part into one of the jambonettes. Sew it up, using a white thread.

3. Heat 2 tablespoons of the butter or corn oil in one large 12-inch skillet or two small skillets. Brown the meat very well until dark golden. Discard the browning fat. Salt and pepper well and add the broth and coriander powder and cook covered until tender, or 25 to 30 minutes. When the chicken is done, remove it to a plate and keep it warm. Sprinkle it with the fresh coriander and serve.

Boning Chicken Legs •••

1. Choose very large chicken legs, absolutely whole ones with all their skin on. You may want to choose what in supermarkets is sold in trays as "leg quarters" so you have a maximum of skin.

2. Put the leg on a chopping board skin down, so the inside of the thigh, which is skinless, faces you.

3. Cut along the whole length of the leg so you expose the thigh, then the drumstick bones.

4. Once the bone is exposed, slide your paring knife blade under the bone to separate the meat. Be careful when you reach the knee joint, for there is no meat, only skin. You have to proceed very carefully so as not to make a hole, which will cause you problems later.

5. When you reach the end of the drumstick, do not cut the skin away from the bone. Turn the piece of meat over so its skin is now facing you and flip all the meat over the end of the drumstick. With a large chef's knife or a cleaver, smartly cut the bone that now sticks out.

6. Now your chicken leg is ready to be stuffed. It can be filled with anything you like: mushrooms, nuts, ham, leftover sausage or meat loaf, cheese, breadcrumbs. Enjoy yourself and be creative. Here is the perfect way to use all your leftovers!

7. One last step: Shape the leg around the stuffing and sew it closed with white thread and a large needle. You will immediately understand the French name *jambonette,* since the piece of chicken will look like a miniature ham.

CHICKEN STEW OR FRICASSEE

A chicken stew in the United States tends to be plain boiled chicken with vegetables and often a flavorful but thin stock. I come from a long line of chicken stewers who always preached to me against a thin or, as they called it, a "long" sauce. Great cooks, goes the saying in France, are short in sauce—and of course I tend to agree personally with this statement even if it is sometimes an arbitrary one.

There is also that question of name, as *stew* sounds rather plain and unsophisticated. Mention the word *fricassee* and everyone's ears perk up. Well, a fricassee is nothing but a chicken stew and in my native cuisine it comes in two shades: white with a white sauce in which the meat is barely colored during searing, and brown with a brown sauce, in which case the meat is deeply browned with searing. This technique is very adaptable and you can vary the searing process as you like to obtain the color you desire.

In modern cuisine, the meat is no longer floured before being seared, because the skin is removed before searing for dietary reasons and for taste. Since the process involves cooking the meat completely immersed in stock, the skin used to remain somewhat rough and unattractive to the tastebuds. On the other hand, the meat would be stringy and overboiled if you waited for the skin to soften completely.

DARK MEAT CHICKEN FRICASSEE WITH DILL AND LEMON

Serves 6

FOR THE
FRICASSEE
6 chicken legs cut into drumsticks and thighs
   Salt and pepper (from the mill)
2 tablespoons butter or oil
3 to 4 cups chicken broth
   Large bouquet of parsley and dill stems
1 bay leaf
1 fresh sprig or ¼ teaspoon dried thyme
1 onion
2 cloves
1 small carrot, cut into 1-inch chunks

FOR THE SAUCE
 3 egg yolks
   Juice of 1 or 2 lemons (to personal taste)
⅓ cup chopped dill weed

1. Season the chicken pieces well with salt and pepper. Heat butter or oil in one large 12-inch skillet or two small skillets, and sauté the chicken pieces until well browned. Discard the browning fat. Add the chicken broth (enough to cover the meat), the bouquet of stems, bay leaf, thyme, the onion stuck with the cloves, and the carrot. Bring to a boil, then turn down to a simmer, and cover the pot, leaving the lid slightly askew. Cook until the chicken is tender or a maximum of 30 minutes.

2. When the meat is cooked, remove the skin and transfer the chicken pieces to a fireproof serving casserole. Keep warm.

3. Quickly reduce the cooking juices by half (to about 1½ cups). Pour 1 cup of this broth through a strainer over chicken and vegetables. Mix the remaining half-cup of broth in the pot with the egg yolks and the juice of one lemon. Place the casserole over medium low heat; shaking it back and forth to keep the meat and vegetables moving constantly, add the egg yolk and lemon liaison until the short sauce coats meat and vegetables (approximately 3 to 4 minutes). Add the dill and mix well. Correct the final seasonings with salt, pepper, and more lemon juice if desired.

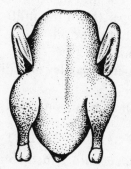

VEGETABLE ACCOMPANIMENTS FOR CHICKEN

Although many chicken dishes come with their own built-in vegetable garnishes, I thought you would enjoy a few combinations that have proved extremely delicious and successful with my own chicken dinners.

GRILLED BUTTERNUT SQUASH AND RUTABAGA

Serves 6

This is good with grilled chicken cutlets. Grill both meat and vegetables together to avoid heating the grill twice. You can also sauté these vegetables.

12 slices of butternut squash, ¼-inch thick and peeled
12 slices of rutabaga, approximately ¼-inch thick and peeled
2 tablespoons of butter or oil, or a mixture of half of each
Salt
Pepper from the mill

1. Parboil the butternut squash slices for 1 minute and the rutabaga slices for 2 to 3 minutes in salted boiling water.

2. Coat the slices of vegetable well with butter or oil and grill them a few minutes on each side at the edges of the grill to avoid their attaching to the surface of the grill. Salt and pepper them and serve with Grilled Chicken Cutlets (see page 11) and Cranberry Compote (see page 12).

WILTED MUSTARD GREENS AND CHERRY TOMATOES

Serves 4 to 6

The mustard greens can be replaced with spinach if you prefer. To wilt the greens, use two wooden spatulas to toss them quickly in the hot fat. Professional cooks with heat-toughened hands do this operation without spatulas.

1	pound mustard greens or spinach
2 to 3	tablespoons butter or oil
	Salt and pepper
12	very ripe cherry tomatoes

1. After you have carefully cleaned and removed the stems of the greens, wash them well and blot them dry in a large towel. Leave a bit of moisture on them; the steam it will produce while you stir-fry will wilt the vegetables.

2. Heat half the butter or oil in a 10-inch skillet. Add the greens, and using your spatulas, quickly turn the greens in the hot butter until heated through. The leaves will lose their stiffness and rigidity. Salt and pepper, and place a large serving of leaves on a platter.

3. In the same skillet, quickly roll the cherry tomatoes on high heat until heated through. Salt and pepper and transfer quickly to the same plate as the greens.

STIR-FRIED ZUCCHINI AND HAZELNUTS

Serves 4 to 6

Excellent with all very plain chicken cutlets.

> ½ cup peeled, coarsely chopped hazelnuts
> 2 tablespoons butter or oil
> 6 narrow baby zucchini, unpeeled, cut in ⅛-inch slices
> Salt
> Pepper from the mill

1. Heat the hazelnuts and butter slowly together in a large skillet until the hazelnuts start browning.

2. Raise the heat, add the zucchini slices and toss a few minutes until the vegetables turn bright green. Salt and pepper well. Serve immediately.

SAUTÉED GREEN BEANS IN BASIL BUTTER

Serves 4 to 6

For virtually all chicken dishes, especially roasters or roasted parts.

> 1 pound green beans, as young as possible
> 4 tablespoons butter at room temperature
> 2 tablespoons finely scissored basil leaves, or 1 teaspooon of dried basil

1. Bring a large pot of water to a boil. Salt it with ½ teaspoon of salt per quart of water. Add the green beans and cook at a rolling boil until tender and bright green, 4 to 6 minutes (avoid grassy-tasting beans, which are undercooked). Drain well.

2. Melt butter in a skillet and add green beans; stir until heated through. Season with basil and salt and pepper.

STIR-FRIED CARROTS AND ZUCCHINI WITH DILL

Serves 4 to 6

Excellent with all types of chicken dishes, these look like brightly colored noodles.

> 4 large carrots, peeled and washed
> 4 large zucchini, unpeeled and washed
> 2 tablespoons butter or oil
>   Salt
>   Pepper
> 2 tablespoons chopped fresh dill or 1 teaspoon dried

1. Set each carrot and zucchini on a chopping board, and using a potato peeler, shave $\frac{1}{16}$-inch thick, $\frac{3}{4}$-inch long strips from all vegetables until you reach the woody centers of the carrots or the seedy centers of the zucchini.

2. Bring a pot of water to boil and add the carrot curls only. Bring back to a boil and then immediately drain the vegetables and rinse them under cold water to stop them from cooking further. Pat them dry.

3. Heat the butter or oil in a skillet, add the carrot curls, toss them into the butter, add the zucchini curls. Salt and pepper. Toss well until the vegetables just start to soften and are heated through. Add the dill.

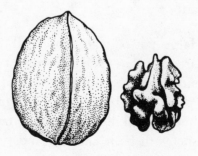

CELERY, RAISINS AND WALNUTS

Serves 4 to 6

For all chicken dishes presented during the winter months.

5 large ribs of celery
2 tablespoons butter
¼ cup dark raisins, soaked 1 hour in lukewarm water
¼ cup chopped walnuts
Salt
Pepper from the mill
2 tablespoons chopped parsley

1. Peel the celery ribs of all their superficial fibers. Cut the ribs across into ⅛-inch thick half-moons. Blanch them for 1 minute in boiling salted water so they turn bright green. Drain well. Pat dry.

2. Heat the butter in a skillet; add the celery, the raisins, and the chopped walnuts, salt and pepper. Toss in the hot butter until well heated through. Add the parsley, salt and pepper and serve quickly.

JULIENNE OF CELERY ROOT

Serves 4 to 6

Celery root is now available in supermarkets and from greengrocers all through the fall, winter and early spring. It is the perfect vegetable to roll into any chicken gravy or sauce. It looks like a large, irregular brown root and is often called celeriac. Discard any spongy part at the center of large roots.

2 medium celery roots, sliced
2 quarts water
2 tablespoons lemon juice
2 tablespoons oil
2 tablespoons flour
Salt
Pepper

1. Pare away the outer skin and cut the celery root into ½-by-½-inch sticks. Turn the angles of the sticks with a paring knife so the pieces of vegetable can roll easily in the chicken gravy.

2. Mix the cold water, lemon juice, oil and flour in a large pot. Stir to mix and bring to a boil, stirring. Add the celery root and cook for 2 minutes. Drain and rinse under cold water and then roll into any good hot chicken gravy or sauce.

STEAK AND POTATOES

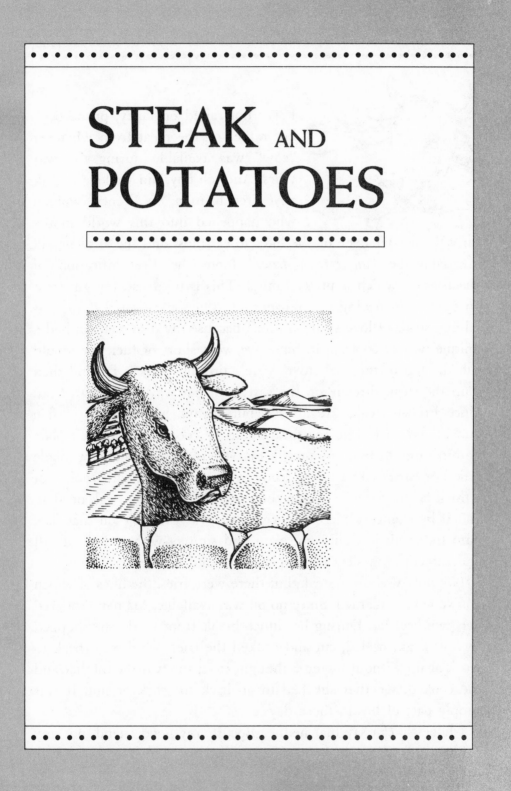

I was not raised on fancy, prime beef, but rather on the meat from whatever "cow" was available during the war years. And, oh boy, did we love it. Ask any French man or French woman who happened into this world in the early thirties what he or she likes to eat most and the answer will invariably be *"un bifteck frites"* (note the Frenchification of "beefsteak," which is pretty funny). This is my treat, my gut treat on days I am feeling unsophisticated. (On sophisticated days, it is salmon steak.) I love steak so much because my dear Maman had a unique way of cooking it. Since we were short of fuel, she would rub the top of the coal stove with a tiny bit of beef fat and then slam the steak directly on the cast iron that was white with heat. Since French steaks are always, but always, a maximum of five ounces and very thin, the meat could be cooked and onto a plate within three to four minutes, a marvelous piece of *araignée* (blade stake) or *onglet* (skirt steak) ready to eat. Often Maman would put a thick layer of coarse salt on the stove and cook the steak on that, and if by chance a piece of nice butter was available on that day, onto the steak it would go, plain and simple, with a dash of salt and sometimes a slew of pepper, fresh and coarse.

Not only was there steak, but there were fries, the likes of which you've never dreamed. Since no oil was available, Maman rendered her own beef fat. During her lunch break from work, she shopped for the steak, peeled, cut and cooked the fries—and went back to work again without giving a thought to it; she was the mother and she cooked, whether she had to go back to work or not. It was simply part of life in those days.

I honestly can say that neither Bocuse, my good friend, nor any other chef, male or female, can cook a steak better than Maman, for she is still alive in a Paris suburb.

Oh, she has had competition over the years, like that wonderful American woman in Strawberry Point, Iowa, who served my family a wonderfully browned steak with baked potatoes and home-baked bread on a still and silent summer night. Bless her soul, she even asked us if we would prefer "boughten" bread! And also the lady who cooks a mean steak and even meaner French fries at the Calypso Café in Annecy, France, just at the edge of the lake. And there's the chef at the Café de Paris in Geneva. Don't miss it; people will send you all over Geneva for a nouvelle cuisine dinner, but Geneva is a mecca for solid, classic foods, prepared in the old-fashioned style. The sauce, the steak and the fries at the Café de Paris are classics; try them after a transatlantic flight as a first contact with Europe—you will never forget them.

In this chapter you will find recipes for steak and potatoes ranging from quick, easy and inexpensive all the way up to elegant and elaborate. There are tips for selecting different cuts of steak, the best way to cook them, and recipes for accompanying sauces and potato side dishes for each steak meal.

CHOOSING STEAKS

Prime meats cost a true fortune nowadays and are becoming less and less popular with the modern awareness of nutrition. All in all, it is best to buy choice meats rather than prime. Since American beef is scientifically raised, there is almost no chance you will ever have a tough piece of steak, whether you choose choice or prime.

LUXURY

Tenderloin: The most tender cut of beef. Available whole as center cut. Sometimes in cryovac (vacuum sealed and packaged in heavy plastic).

Chateaubriand: The head of tenderloin, weighing about 2 pounds.

Look for steaks no more than ¾ inch thick, 3 to 4 ounces trimmed, for a single portion. Choose steaks with little marbling. Individual steaks are sometimes labeled "tournedos" (so called because they are supposed to be so tender you can cook them in the time it takes you to turn your back, or in French, *tourner dos*).

EXPENSIVE

Sirloin Strip, Rib and Porterhouse Steak: Tastiest of all meats. Can be cut to weigh as little as 8 ounces or as much as 28 ounces. A 10-ounce, ¾-inch-thick steak is a reasonable portion, which will weigh about 7 ounces after trimming.

AFFORDABLE

Sirloin: Less tender than luxury steaks. Quite lean, very tasty but less tender than tenderloin or rib. Can be cut into large ½-inch-thick steaks for family.

Chicken or Blade: ½ to ¾ inch thick, 3½ to 5 ounces untrimmed and 2½ to 3½ ounces after trimming. Excellent taste, less tender. Often sold in family-pack trays. Cut out of the shoulder or chuck of beef.

Skirt Steaks: Newly discovered for its taste. Often wrongly labeled in our supermarkets as "flank steak." This cut is popular in Tex-Mex and Chinese cooking and in New York, where it is sold as Roumanian tenderloin. Can be purchased whole or cut on the bias (diagonally across the piece of meat) into individual steaks.

Eye of the Round: Only moderately tasty but best for persons on low-fat diets.

THE TECHNIQUES OF COOKING STEAKS

Panfrying

Panfrying is by far the fastest and also the easiest way to cook a steak, truly a matter of one, two, three steps, which end in a tasty piece of meat. All you need is a frying pan or skillet that conducts the heat very well. The best skillet is an old-fashioned, well-seasoned cast-iron one, nice and black with age. But anything with a thick bottom will do just as well.

Tenderloin, blade, skirt steaks, porterhouse and rib steaks can all be used for panfrying.

CLASSIC PANFRIED STEAK WITH RED WINE SAUCE

Serves 4

Here is a recipe to practice on. A nice variation of steak and onions.

> 4 blade or skirt steaks
> 2 tablespoons polyunsaturated oil
> Salt
> Freshly ground pepper
> ¼ cup finely chopped scallions, white part only
> ⅔ cup dry red wine
> Dash each cinnamon and ground cloves
> 2 tablespoons butter, or less to taste

1. Trim the steaks of all fat. Heat oil in a large skillet over medium high heat. Add the steaks to the pan and sear well on one side to develop a good crust, nice and brown. This will send the juices of the meat upward. Now turn the meat over and sear the second side exactly as you did the first. Salt and pepper the already seared side and wait for the meat juices to bead nice and red on the seared surface. At this point, the steak is done rare and ready to be served if you like that degree of doneness. If you like it medium rare, turn the steak over once more and cook it 1 or 2 minutes longer. Season the second side of the steak. To check doneness of the steak, press on the meat with your fingertip: the meat gives readily under the finger if rare, is a bit more resistant if medium rare, and is hard and resists your finger if you have overcooked it.

2. Remove the steaks from the skillet; add the scallions to the pan and cook for 1 to 2 minutes, or until lightly browned. Add the wine and cook down until almost no liquid remains. Add cinnamon and cloves to the skillet along with the butter and shake pan back and forth until butter has melted.

3. To serve: Cut meat into thick slices and spoon sauce over them. Accompany with Rissolé Potatoes (page 55), which are wonderful when rolled in the red wine sauce.

Pan Roasting

Pan roasting is a first cousin to panfrying, and is especially designed to prepare cuts of steak or first-quality tender meats 1½ to 2 inches thick. This method is best applied to the center cut of the tenderloin, to thick rib or sirloin strip steaks and sirloin steak, as well as to the shoulder steaks often sold as "London broil" in supermarkets.

PAN-ROASTED TENDERLOIN WITH RED WINE BÉARNAISE

Serves 4 to 6

A modern technique for cooking a thick steak, combined with a modern version of the classic, wonderful béarnaise sauce. Begin by making the sauce. The meat juices that are left behind in the skillet are added to the sauce to tie together all the flavors.

> 1 2-pound piece of center cut of tenderloin (Chateaubriand)
> 2 tablespoons butter or oil
> Salt and pepper
> 3 to 4 tablespoons water
> 1 recipe Red Wine Béarnaise Sauce (below)

1. Trim the meat of all fat. Heat oil or butter in a large skillet or pan. Sear the first surface of the meat as well as its sides all around. Turn the meat over; season well while the second side is searing. Turn over again and season the second side, staying on high heat.

2. So far nothing differs from panfrying the steak. But things now change as you reduce the heat to medium and keep turning the piece of meat every 3 to 4 minutes for the next 10 minutes. Finally, take a lid one or two sizes smaller than your pan and push it down on the meat until the lid becomes nice and hot (be sure to use a pot holder when doing this). This forces the heat to the middle of the meat to dispatch any bluish rare center. Salt and pepper the roast abundantly again, and then remove it from the pan. Discard the fat in the pan. Deglaze the pan well with the water, scraping to dissolve all the solidified meat juices, and cook to reduce until only 1 to 2 tablespoons remain. Strain these juices into a béarnaise sauce to connect the flavor of the meat with the sauce.

RED WINE BÉARNAISE SAUCE

Yield: 1 generous cup

For 125 years everyone has made béarnaise sauce with white wine and vinegar—why not be a bit different?

    3 shallots, chopped extremely finely
    2 tablespoons red wine vinegar
    ½ cup dry red wine
    2 tablespoons each chopped chervil and tarragon stems, or
       2 teaspoons each dried
    ¾ teaspoon coarsely cracked white peppercorns
       Small bouquet garni of 5 parsley stems, ½ bay leaf and a
       sprig of thyme
    ⅛ teaspoon salt
    2 egg yolks
    ½ pound melted, unsalted butter, barely warm
       Lukewarm salted water
   1½ tablespoons each chopped chervil and tarragon leaves, or
       1½ tablespoons of fresh parsley

1. In a heavy pot, mix shallots, red wine vinegar, red wine, chervil and tarragon stems, pepper, bouquet garni and salt. Bring to a boil, turn down heat and cook until the mixture is reduced to 2 tablespoons of solids and liquids together. Turn the heat off. Have a small wire whisk ready. Add the egg yolks one at a time. The heat in the pot will cook the egg yolks. As soon as the first yolk hits the bottom of the pan start whisking very quickly with a small whisk. Whisk until the egg yolk has turned pale yellow and very thick. Then whisk in the melted butter tablespoon by tablespoon until all the butter has been absorbed. If the sauce seems too thick, add an occasional half

teaspoon of salted water. Place the chopped chervil and tarragon leaves in a clean small pot and strain the sauce over the herbs. Stir well. Keep the sauce warm on the side of the stove while you prepare the meat.

2. Trim the meat. Heat the oil or butter in a large skillet. Sear the first surface of the meat as well as its sides all around. Turn the meat over, season the seared side well while the second side is searing; turn over again and season the second side, staying on high heat. When the meat is done to your taste, remove it to a platter, slice crosswise into slices ¼ inch thick and serve with the red wine béarnaise.

NOTE: To tie together the flavor of the sauce and the meat, add reserved meat juices to the béarnaise after you've made the steaks.

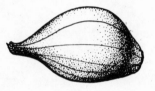

Salt-Pan Broiling

Known in French as *"à la croque-au-sel,"* this method of cooking steaks is the favorite of the French. It is best used for a relatively thin steak, barely one-half inch thick and preferably cut from a very large rib eye. Tenderloin, sirloin strip or the other affordable steaks are never as tasty as a rib eye steak when prepared this way.

SALT-PAN BROILED STEAK, BISTRO-STYLE

Serves 4

> 4 rib eye steaks, about ½ inch thick
> Kosher or coarse salt
> Butter or Diet Butter

1. Trim the steaks. Pour a layer ⅛ inch thick of kosher or coarse salt into a skillet to cover its bottom completely and very evenly. As the salt heats, it will literally start jumping from the bottom of the pan. At this point, add the steaks and sear them well on high heat. Allow to cook for 2 minutes. Your steak will be seared by the intense heat accumulated in the crystals of salt, and patches of very heavily browned meat will be visible as you turn it over. Obviously, you need not salt the already seared surface; proceed to sear the second side. The meat will be succulent between its two salty surfaces.

2. No sauce is needed. However, for a hint more flavor: either a pad of cool, unsalted butter or a wedge of lemon. You can also serve Diet Butter (see below).

DIET BUTTER

Yields about 1½ cups

This is the closest dieters can come to eating regular butter. The flavor is almost as delicious, and there are a lot fewer calories.

    ½ pound unsalted butter
    ½ cup buttermilk
    1 cup polyunsaturated oil
    4 capsules lecithin (available in health food stores)

1. Put the butter in a food processor or electric mixer, cream well.

2. Gradually add the buttermilk and then the oil and beat or process until homogenous.

3. Cut open lecithin capsules and dribble the contents into the butter mixture. Mix or process again for another 15 seconds.

4. Store in a covered plastic container. Keep refrigerated. Mixture will last several weeks.

Stove-Top Grilling

Grilling steaks indoors can be done on the good old American cast-iron griddle to achieve that outdoor look. If available, a ribbed griddle allows any fat from the steak to fall away from the meat. Tenderloin, porterhouse, sirloin tip, rib steak, blade are all good steaks for grilling.

MICHAEL'S GRILLED STEAK

Serves 4

Here is my friend Michael Bauer's recipe for thick grilled steak. This can be made with the center cut of tenderloin, a rib steak to serve 3 to 4 persons, or a London broil cut from the chuck or the top round of the beef.

> 1 large 1½-inch-thick shoulder or top round London broil
> 1 tablespoon dark soy sauce
> 1 piece ginger, the size of a quarter, peeled
> 1 tablespoon oil
> 1½ tablespoons butter
> ¼ cup superfinely slivered scallion greens

1. Trim the steak of all outside fat and gristle.

2. Put the soy sauce in a small bowl and grate the ginger finely into it. Brush the mixture over the meat and let stand at room temperature on a stainless-steel rack for 2 hours.

3. Heat the grill over medium high flame. Lightly oil the surface of the grill. Wipe off any excess oil with paper towels.

4. Add the steaks and sear for 2 minutes on the first side. Turn over, salt and pepper the seared side and watch for blood to bead on its surface.

5. When the meat is seared on both sides, it is "blue," that is to say, very rare between the two seared crusts, and must be slowly forced to absorb the heat to continue cooking to the center. Use a large lid that will cover the meat well. Push the lid down on the meat to force the heat through it. Reduce the heat to moderate. Cook for another 8 minutes. Season the meat again when done and serve in paper-thin slices. Serve with Stock or Cream Potato Gratin (see pages 58 and 59).

GRILLED STEAK WITH WALNUT AND ROQUEFORT BUTTER

Serves 6

> 1 recipe Walnut and Roquefort Butter (see opposite)
> 1 tablespoon oil
> 6 ½-inch-thick tenderloin, sirloin strip, or large blade steaks
> Salt and pepper

1. Prepare Walnut and Roquefort Butter according to the directions opposite.

2. Trim steaks of all fat.

3. Heat the grill over a medium high flame. Lightly oil the surface of the grill. Wipe off any excess oil with paper towels.

4. Add the steaks and sear for 2 minutes on the first side. Turn over, salt and pepper the seared side and watch for blood to bead on its surface. If you like your steak rare, sear and season the second side. Serve. If you prefer it medium rare, turn it over once more and cook it for 2 more minutes while you season its second side.

5. Top each steak with one or two thin slices of the compound butter. As a vegetable, use Red Parsleyed Potatoes Cooked in Broth (see page 57).

WALNUT AND ROQUEFORT BUTTER

Yield: approximately ½ cup

⅛ teaspoon meat extract
½ cup dry red wine
1 large shallot, chopped very finely
Pinch of dried thyme
Salt
Pepper from the mill
¼ cup unsalted butter, room temperature
2 teaspoons chopped walnuts
2 tablespoons chopped parsley
1½ tablespoons Roquefort or Stilton cheese

1. Mix meat extract, wine, shallot, thyme and a pinch of salt and pepper and reduce completely over medium low heat, until absolutely no liquid is left in the saucepan. Cool completely.

2. Mash the butter with a fork or knife blade and gradually work into it the cooled shallot mixture, the walnuts, the parsley and the Roquefort or Stilton. Mash well until completely mixed. Shape into a sausage, using a piece of clear plastic, and refrigerate until solid. Store leftover butter in your freezer.

Broiling

Always preheat your broiler, and remember that the door of the oven must remain ajar all the while that your meat is broiling. Shoulder steaks, top round, London broil, tenderloin are good cuts of meat for broiling.

VENISONED STEAK

Serves 4 to 6

Since there is very little venison left in some parts of this country, one can simulate the taste with steaks by leaving them for several days in a cooked marinade of wine, spirits and aromatics. This marination gives the meat a taste that is evocative of the taste of wild game.

FOR THE MARINADE
2 cups dry red wine (Côtes du Rhône or Zinfandel)
1 onion, finely chopped
2 shallots, finely chopped
8 juniper berries, crushed
Sprig of fresh thyme or 1 teaspoon dried
1 bay leaf, crushed
1 tablespoon chopped parsley stems
1 ounce gin

FOR THE STEAK AND SMALL GRAVY
1 large shoulder or top round London broil, or 1 to 1½ pounds center cut of tenderloin, approximately ¾ inch thick
½ cup beef stock or broth
1 tablespoon oil
Salt and pepper
1½ tablespoons unsalted butter
½ teaspoon coarsely cracked pepper

1. Place wine, onion, shallots, crushed juniper berries, thyme, crushed bay leaf and parsley stems in a saucepan and cook until it has reduced to 1 cup. Add gin and cook for 3 minutes more. Cool completely.

2. Completely remove all traces of fat and gristle from the outside of the meat. Pour half the marinade into a large glass baking dish. Add the meat and cover it with the remainder of the marinade. Wrap it in plastic wrap. Let the meat marinate for 2 to 4 days, turning it occasionally.

3. Remove the meat from the marinade. Pour marinade into a saucepan and cook to reduce to ½ cup. Mix with the stock or broth.

4. Pat the meat dry with paper towels and brush it with the oil. Set the meat on a rack placed over a roasting pan. Place the pan and rack 4 inches below the heat element. Sear well on the first side, salt and pepper, turn over the meat, sear it on the second side and season it. If your steak is ½ to ¾ inch thick, it will be rare by the time you have seared both sides.

5. When the meat is done to your liking, deglaze the roasting pan with the mixture of marinade and broth and cook down to ½ cup. Strain into a sauce boat and add the butter and cracked pepper. Mix well. Serve the sauce on the sliced meat. Serve with Swiss Baked Potatoes (see page 56).

POTATOES

To make a sublime steak dinner even more heavenly, all you need are potatoes. There are as many varieties of potatoes as there are steaks. Some are best baked, others fried, and still others boiled or baked in a liquid. Any of these recipes can be paired with any of the steak recipes in this chapter.

RISSOLÉ POTATOES

Serves 4 to 6

For this side dish, Maine-grown potatoes or California new potatoes are best. You need a 10-inch skillet and a 10-inch or larger cake pan.

    4 potatoes, peeled and cut into ¾-inch cubes
¼ cup oil
    Salt
    Freshly ground pepper
    Chopped parsley

    1. Wash the potato cubes three times under cold water and pat them dry completely in a tea towel.

    2. Heat the oil in the skillet at high heat until it starts rippling. Add the potatoes. Toss them well in the hot oil to build a crust all around each piece.

    3. Turn the heat down to medium and continue to toss the potatoes at regular intervals for about 15 minutes or until well browned on all sides and the tip of a knife goes in easily.

4. There are two ways to finish the potatoes: either raise the heat again and let the potatoes color to a deep golden or transfer the potatoes and their oil to a cake pan and finish browning them in a preheated 375° oven.

5. To serve, remove the potatoes from the oil with a slotted spoon and drain them on paper towels. Salt and pepper, sprinkle with parsley.

SWISS BAKED POTATOES

Serves 6

This is the Swiss version of the good old American baked stuffed potato. Use Idaho or new California baking potatoes.

    6 large baking potatoes
    ¾ cup coarsely grated Gruyère or ordinary Swiss cheese
⅓ to ½ cup heavy cream
    ¼ teaspoon freshly grated nutmeg
    1 clove garlic, mashed
   1½ tablespoons chopped parsley
    ½ cup butter, melted
      Salt and pepper

1. Scrub the potatoes, prick them with a skewer and bake them for 1 hour in a preheated 400° oven.

2. While the potatoes are baking, combine the grated cheese, cream, nutmeg, garlic, and parsley. Set aside.

3. When the potatoes are done, remove from oven (do not turn off) and cut lids in the tops. With a spoon, scoop out the inside of each potato and place in a bowl. Add the melted butter. Mix well, season with salt and pepper.

4. Stuff each potato with an equal amount of half the buttered potato mixture. Add ⅙ of the cream and cheese mixture to each. Stuff with the remaining buttered potato mixture.

5. Return the potatoes to oven and bake until the top of each one is golden and crusty, about 5 to 7 minutes.

RED PARSLEYED POTATOES
COOKED IN BROTH

Serves 4 to 6

The best potatoes to use here are red Bliss potatoes as small as
possible. Cut larger potatoes into small pieces and trim the angles of
each piece to prevent them from breaking off and surrounding the
vegetables with mush.

> 1 pound very small red potatoes, peeled
> 2 cups chicken or beef broth
> Salt
> Pepper from the mill
> 2 tablespoons butter, or Diet Butter (see page 50)
> Chopped parsley

1. Place potatoes, broth, salt, pepper and butter in a large
saucepan. Slowly bring to a boil, then turn down to a simmer. Cook,
covered, until the potatoes are tender and have absorbed almost all of
the broth. Serve promptly sprinkled with chopped parsley.

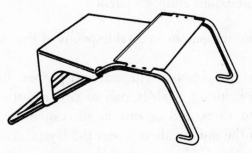

Potato Gratins

Scalloped potatoes are gratins, and whether they are prepared with
cream or with broth, they are downright sinfully good! The best in-
strument to slice the potatoes? A food processor if you own one, of
course, but a good old Feemster potato slicer that costs around three

dollars does just as well; just slow down toward the end of the potato so as not to add fingertip slices to your dish.

For my gratins I like to use a good Maine or Prince Edward Island potato. Of course, the Idaho bakers can be used also.

STOCK POTATO GRATIN

Serves 4 to 6

 6 onions, thinly sliced
 5 tablespoons butter or oil
 6 large Maine potatoes, peeled and sliced into ⅛-inch slices
   Salt
   Freshly ground pepper
2 to 3 cups chicken or beef broth
 ½ cup fresh breadcrumbs
 1 clove garlic
 2 tablespoons chopped parsley

1. Sauté the onions in 3 tablespoons of the butter or oil until translucent.

2. Toss the potatoes with salt and pepper. Butter or oil a 1-quart baking dish, using 1 tablespoon of either butter or oil, and arrange the potato slices and onions in successive layers: half of the potatoes, half of the onions, then repeat the layers. Add the broth and bake in a preheated 325° oven until the potatoes have softened, approximately 30 minutes.

3. Sprinkle the potatoes with the crumbs mixed with the garlic and parsley. Sprinkle the top of the dish evenly with the remaining 2 tablespoons of butter or oil, and bake until golden. The total baking time is in the vicinity of 1 hour. The dish is done when the tip of a paring knife meets no resistance going through the potato slices and the broth has been totally absorbed.

CREAM POTATO GRATIN

Serves 6

1 large clove garlic
2 tablespoons butter
6 medium Maine potatoes
   Salt
   Pepper from the mill
½ teaspoon freshly grated nutmeg, or to taste
2 cups heavy cream, lightly salted

1. Crush the garlic clove and rub a 1½-quart baking dish with it. Pick out and discard any pieces of garlic from the dish and let the garlic juice dry on the dish's surface.

2. Butter the dish with the full 2 tablespoons of butter. Place the sliced potatoes in a large bowl, then salt, pepper and nutmeg them.

3. Transfer the potatoes into the baking dish in three layers, and top each layer with about one-third of the cream. Shake the dish well.

4. Bake in a slow, preheated 325° oven for 30 minutes. Break the crust of cream. Bake for another 15 minutes and break the newly formed crust again. Finally, finish baking until the surface of the potatoes is deep golden.

NOTE: This dish keeps for hours in a 140° oven, and leftovers can be used for rich home fries within the next two days.

GRAINS

GRAINS FOR MEATLESS MEALS

At age six, I thought breakfast consisted of very pale café au lait accompanied by *pain grillé,* slices of toasted French bread, that my dear great-grandmother, whom I loved more than anyone, called *rôties. Rôties* were served smothered with wonderful fresh butter from Charente and great globs of homemade jams of all sorts. I called my great-grandmother Mimi. She had a garden that was squeezed between two rows of apartment buildings, and from it she would pluck apricots, red and black currants, rhubarb, baby strawberries and gooseberries and, in order of ripening, simmer them in the big copper jam kettle and pack them into pots sealed with paraffin. Those were the jams that ultimately would arrive on my bread and butter.

In 1936, while I was away on a trip with my parents, Mimi died suddenly. Her death seemed to mark the end of the good life of prewar days in France.

Unlike Mimi, my mother, for one reason or another, was always concerned about my being skinny, and began to feed me *des flocons d'avoine.* Oh-la-la, what a shock. The fancy name stands for oatmeal porridge. The first time that concoction landed on my breakfast plate, I rebelled. The porridge was filmy, sticky, too hot, it burned the mouth, and as it cooled it sat there like a lump of gray matter quite horrible to look at. Oh, where were Mimi's *rôties?* A friend from Brittany came to my rescue, telling my mother to sweeten the offending mush with applesauce or honey or even cut-up fresh fruit. To her, oatmeal was the staple of life, and she made sure that I would enjoy it. I soon discovered other things that improved oatmeal: cinnamon, all the sweet spices, and that wonderful combination of salted butter and sugar. We continued eating quite a bit of oatmeal during the war years, but as soon as we could go back to our *rôties* and jam after 1945 we sure did, and fast.

Only the poor kids who were looked after by English nannnies (and there were still quite a few in school until the early fifties), were stuck with the oatmeal. In 1944, when Camembert came back, I took to it rather rapidly. Since I was trained as a runner in those days and needed tons of calories, I would bring with me from home a healthy slice of bread and Camembert to supplement the lean school lunch. Would you believe that one of the nanny kids offered me five francs, a fortune at the time, for my one-ounce piece of Camembert? Hey, for a kid on oatmeal, boiled meat and vegetables, the cheese was a treat. I bought her a whole cheese with the five francs, and it stank up the gym locker room for four days.

Many years later the hard winters of New England would quickly show me the value of a bowl of steaming hot oatmeal, and my own children helped complete my education in grains. They are Appalachian Mountain Club kids, and in those huts up there in the White Mountains, they cook and bake with more grains than I have ever seen. They have a tendency to be vegetarians, and their food, when they finally get down to cooking it for me, very much resembles the natural foods of the sixties. They keep vegetarian cookbooks like *The Enchanted Broccoli Forest* on their night tables. Because of them, I have gotten used to grain and cereals—quite happily, I should say.

Many people have opposite reactions to grains: either they love them or, as I did originally, they loathe them. If you are not that fond of grains, remember one thing: they are the key to being skinny. Look at the Japanese, the Chinese, the Indians and all those tall Armenians. They eat mostly grain, and they certainly are not fat. The grains used in all the recipes that follow are available in the supermarket or in health food and specialty stores.

The recipes for grain in this chapter are organized by cooking technique. You will notice as we go along that with each successive technique, less and less liquid is used for cooking. The result is a drier, lighter, fluffier grain. We begin by cooking grains such as wheat or rice in large amounts of water. These grains are drained, rinsed and tossed in dressings for salads. Next, cornmeal and semolina flour are cooked in slightly less liquid until they become mush. This technique is used to make polenta and gnocchi. Then comes a technique for short-grain rice. By adding small, successive amounts of liquid, the rice becomes a puddinglike, creamy mixture known as risotto. For me this is food for the gods. Then comes a technique for making pilafs that is perfect for wheat as well as rice. Finally, I have developed my own technique for cooking a grain native only to America, wild rice. This new technique keeps the wonderful and unique flavor and texture that wild rice has.

But first, we begin with a recipe for a grain dish that requires no cooking at all.

OATMEAL AND FRESH FRUIT (BIERCHERMUESLI)

Serves 6 to 8

This dish of rolled oats, nuts, fresh and dried fruits is one that I learned from my landlady when I was working in Switzerland as a young woman. Just enough milk is added to refreshen the mixture. I guarantee you that any child will vacuum his plate of it. It is also a wonderful way to use up overripe fruit.

> 3 cups dry oat flakes
> 2½ cups milk
> Honey to taste
> A pinch of salt (optional)
> ⅓ cup raisins
> ½ cup coarsely chopped hazelnuts
> ½ cup strawberries, sliced
> ½ cup blueberries
> ½ cup peeled, cut-up peaches or nectarines
> ½ cup orange sections
> ½ cup grapefruit sections (preferably pink)
> 1 small banana, sliced
> 1 teaspoon grated orange rind
> ½ cup raspberries
> 1 cup heavy cream, whipped (optional)

1. Put the oatmeal flakes in a large bowl. Add the milk, honey, salt, if desired, and the raisins. Soak, covered, overnight in the refrigerator.

2. The next morning, add the chopped nuts and all the remaining ingredients except the raspberries and cream. Top with raspberries.

NOTE: To make more opulent, serve each portion with a large spoonful of whipped cream.

COOKING GRAINS FOR SALADS

Rinse all grains under *warm* water, not cold. Keep rinsing until all traces of starch disappear to prevent the grain particles from sticking to one another. Here is a recipe for a pleasant mixed-grain salad that is strictly vegetarian. Should you decide to make it a grain and protein salad, don't hesitate to add shellfish, meat or cheese to it.

MIXED-GRAIN AND VEGETABLE SALAD

Serves 6

¾ cup millet
¾ cup bulgur wheat
¾ cup brown rice
1 very large red onion, very coarsely chopped
4 tomataoes, peeled, seeded and diced in ⅓-inch cubes
3 small zucchini, seeded and diced in ⅓-inch cubes
2 red peppers, diced in ⅓-inch cubes
2 green peppers, diced in ⅓-inch cubes
2 yellow peppers, diced in ⅓-inch cubes
Salt
Pepper from the mill
Parsley leaves

FOR THE DRESSING
1½ teaspoons Dijon mustard
1 teaspoon salt
½ teaspoon coarsely cracked pepper
¼ teaspoon ground sage
4 tablespoons chopped parsley
1½ teaspoons powdered ginger

½ cup tomato sauce
½ teaspoon red pepper flakes
½ teaspoon dried oregano
⅓ cup red wine vinegar
1 cup virgin olive oil or other oil

1. Bring 2 quarts of water to a boil. Add salt and pepper. Immerse the millet. Simmer, uncovered, for 15 to 20 minutes, or until tender. Drain in a colander placed over a large pot. Keep the water. Rinse the millet under warm water.

2. Repeat the same procedure for the bulgur, cooking it for 25 minutes; add the brown rice, cooking it for 30 minutes (see Note). In a large bowl, mix all the cooked grains together and set aside.

3. If you desire, salt the onion, let it stand for 30 minutes to extract the pungent juices, discard the juices, and add the onion to the vegetables. Stir all the vegetables into the grains. Correct the basic seasoning with salt and pepper.

4. Put all the dressing ingredients into the container of a blender and blend until smooth. Correct the seasoning, if necessary. Toss the grain and vegetable mixture with the dressing. Serve dotted with parsley leaves.

NOTE: There are so many types of brown rice and so many different qualities that the cooking time may vary enormously, depending on the number of sheets of bran left around each grain of rice. As a cook, you will have to decide for yourself when your brown rice is done.

COOKING GRAINS FOR POLENTA OR GNOCCHI

The principle of cooking grains for dishes such as American cornmeal mush or the Italian polentas or gnocchi consists of introducing a rather small amount of grain into a rather large amount of liquid and boiling the mixture, stirring constantly, until the wooden spoon you are using to stir stands by itself in the center of the pot.

POLENTA CONCIA

Serves 6

A *polenta concia* in Italian means one that has been cooked to a mush and then spooned into a dish and rebaked. This marvelous recipe combines polenta with the wonderful taste of mushrooms and Fontina cheese.

FOR THE POLENTA
8 cups cold water
2 cups cornmeal, half finely ground, half coarsely ground
1 teaspoon salt
Pepper from the mill

FOR THE SAUCE
2 onions, chopped
5 tablespoons butter
3 pounds Italian plum tomatoes, peeled, seeded and cut into cubes (if you cannot find fresh tomatoes, use two cans of Italian tomatoes, drained)
Salt
Pepper from the mill
1½ pounds fresh mushrooms of your choice (fresh wild boleti would be wonderful, cleaned and quartered)
2 anchovies, mashed
¼ cup chopped parsley
1 tiny clove garlic, mashed
½ pound Fontina or Gruyère, cut into slivers

1. Bring 5 cups of water to a boil. Reduce to simmer. Mix the cornmeal with 3 cups of cold water. Stirring constantly, add the cold water and cornmeal mixture and salt and pepper to the simmering water and stir until the mixture thickens, about 10 to 15 minutes. Reduce the heat and cook, slowly stirring, over medium heat for 10 to 15 minutes or until a wooden spoon stands in the mixture.

2. *To prepare the sauce:* Sauté the onions in 1½ tablespoons of the butter until translucent. Add the tomatoes, the salt and the pepper and cook until you have a saucelike texture (about 10 min-

utes). Sauté the mushrooms in 2 tablespoons of butter until the juices run out. Add them to the tomato sauce. Resimmer together for 5 to 6 minutes. Add the anchovies, parsley and garlic clove and set aside.

3. Grease a 1½-quart baking dish with the remaining 1½ tablespoons of butter. Add half of the cornmeal; spoon on a layer of half the sauce; add half of the cheese slivers. Add the remainder of the polenta. Top it with the remainder of the sauce and cheese and bake in a preheated 350° oven for 25 minutes until the cheese browns slightly. Make sure to cool a bit before serving. Cut into squares and serve with a crisp green salad.

CORN GRITS WITH OKRA AND SQUASHED TOMATOES

Serves 6

Here's a dish that features grits, for a luncheon or as a side dish with dinner.

         ½ cup butter
         4 shallots, chopped finely
     1½ cups coarse corn grits
5½ to 6 cups water or light broth
         Salt
         Pepper from the mill
         1 pound okra, cleaned
         2 tablespoons butter or oil
         2 pounds fresh sun-ripened Italian plum tomatoes, peeled, seeded and coarsely chopped, or 1 large can of Italian tomatoes, drained
         ½ teaspoon dried hot pepper flakes

1. In a large skillet, heat the butter. Add the shallots and sauté for a few minutes. Add the corn grits and toss in the mixture until hot to the tip of a finger. Add water or broth, salt and pepper. Cover and let cook until all liquid has been absorbed, approximately 20 minutes.

2. While the grits cook, slice the okra in ¼-inch-thick slices and sauté in 2 tablespoons of hot butter or oil until golden. Add the tomatoes, hot pepper and salt and cook until saucelike. Serve over or mixed with the corn pilaf.

VARIATIONS: Cool the pilaf. Beat 1 or 2 eggs and add to the grain. Shape into small ⅓-inch-thick, 3-inch-diameter cakes and fry in butter or oil. Serve topped with the vegetable sauce.

POLENTA WITH SPINACH AND PARMESAN CREAM

Serves 6

In this recipe, the polenta is formed into a thin layer, cooled, and cut into thin rectangles, which are then fried and topped with a delicious cheese sauce.

FOR THE POLENTA
8 cups cold water
2 cups cornmeal, half finely ground, half coarsely ground
Salt
Pepper from the mill
3 tablespoons melted butter or oil

FOR THE SAUCE AND VEGETABLES

2 pounds spinach, cleaned, not completely dried

1½ cups heavy cream

½ to ⅔ cup freshly grated Parmesan cheese

Salt

Pepper, coarsely cracked

Dash grated nutmeg

1. Bring 5 cups of water to a boil. Reduce to a simmer. Mix the cornmeal with 3 cups of cold water. Stirring constantly, add the cold water and cornmeal mixture and salt and pepper to the simmering water and stir until the mixture thickens. Reduce the heat and cook, slowly stirring, until a wooden spoon can stand up in it, about 10 or 15 minutes.

2. Grease a 13-by-18-inch jelly-roll pan and spread the cornmeal mush evenly into the pan. It will be approximately ⅓ to ½ inch thick. Let cool completely. When cool, cut into 12 rectangles.

3. Place the spinach leaves in a large skillet. Cover and steam until they just wilt. Remove spinach and set aside. In the same skillet, add the cream and reduce to 1 cup. Add the Parmesan cheese, salt, if needed, and coarsely cracked pepper.

4. Heat the melted butter in a frying pan or skillet and fry the rectangles on both sides for 2 or 3 minutes, or until golden. Top each crouton with a few spinach leaves and the Parmesan cream. Grate a bit of nutmeg over each portion.

SEMOLINA GNOCCHI WITH RATATOUILLE

Serves 6

Gnocchi is an Italian-style dumpling. This version is made with semolina flour instead of potatoes and makes a delicious entrée when accompanied by ratatouille.

FOR THE GNOCCHI
8 cups cold water
2 cups semolina
1 teaspoon salt
Freshly ground pepper
3 tablespoons melted butter or oil
⅓ to ½ cup grated Pecorino or Romano cheese (optional)

FOR THE RATATOUILLE
3 tablespoons olive oil or other oil
3 cloves garlic, mashed
½ cup parsley
3 large onions, chopped finely
2 green peppers, coarsely diced
2 red peppers, coarsely diced
2 yellow peppers, coarsely diced
2 pounds fresh sun-ripened tomatoes, peeled, seeded and chopped
3 small zucchini, diced
1½ teaspoons dried oregano and basil, mixed
1 bay leaf
Salt
Pepper from the mill

1. Bring 5 cups of water to a boil. Reduce to a simmer. Mix the semolina with 3 cups of cold water. Stirring constantly, add the cold water and semolina mixture and the salt and pepper to the simmering water and stir until the mixture thickens, about 10 to 15 minutes. Reduce the heat and cook, slowly stirring, until a wooden spoon stands in the mixture.

2. Spread cooked semolina onto a greased jelly-roll pan, 13 by 18 inches. Cool completely.

3. In a large skillet, prepare the ratatouille. Heat the oil in the pan. Add the garlic and parsley, and brown very well. Add the onions, and cook until they lose their moisture and start to brown lightly. Add the green peppers. Toss together and cook for 5 minutes. Add the red peppers. Toss together and cook for 5 more minutes. Add the yellow peppers. Toss together and cook for 5 more minutes. Add the tomatoes and mix well; add the zucchini and the remaining seasonings, and cook until the mixture is positively overcooked and resembles a thick relish.

4. Cut the cooled semolina into 12 squares. Melt the 3 tablespoons of butter or oil in a skillet and fry the squares until golden on both sides. Serve them topped with the ratatouille and, if you desire, a sprinkling of Pecorino or Romano cheese.

COOKING SHORT-GRAIN RICE FOR RISOTTO

So far we have cooked grain in a large amount of liquid, or as a mush, forcing the grain to absorb a good amount of liquid. With risotto, you have a new technique, in which you let the rice absorb quite a bit of liquid but not as much as you did before. To cook a good risotto, it is absolutely essential to use short-grain rice. Converted rice is not starchy enough to produce the characteristic puddinglike texture. The basic proportions of a good risotto call for between 3½ and 4½ cups of liquid to each cup of rice. The rice, being flooded by the large amount of liquid, should release just enough of its starch to allow the grains to adhere lightly to one another.

Making a risotto is not all that easy, since no rice will absorb quite the same amount of liquid, so it is up to you to decide when the rice has reached the texture that you like. The best way is to taste it as it cooks. Italians have developed a knack for producing a rice that is still, as they say, *al dente,* and has released just the right amount of starch. My cousin Bruno, who is Milanese by birth, taught me to make risotto properly and forbade me to use a spoon, wooden or otherwise, to stir the water or broth into it. His theory is that it bruises the grains and releases too much starch, making the risotto a sticky mess. I also learned from Bruno that the liquid used to make risotto should be a very light one, not a thick heavy stock which will not penetrate the grains efficiently, and that the key to its taste is a load of butter. The reserved cooking water of any fresh vegetable you have cooked will do just fine. You be the judge as to whether you want to replace the butter with polyunsaturated or olive oil.

VEGETARIAN RISOTTO

Serves 6

This is a vegetarian dinner that is as much a joy to look at as it is to eat.

FOR THE GARNISH
Salt and pepper
½ pound shelled peas
¼ pound green beans, strung and cut slantwise into ½-inch thicknesses
1 pound regular or baby carrots, peeled
1 pound red or white radishes, peeled
3 zucchini
3 small yellow squash
2 tablespoons butter or oil

FOR THE RISOTTO
4½ to 6 cups very light chicken broth or vegetable cooking water
½ cup butter or oil
3 large onions, very finely minced, about 3 cups
1½ cups Italian arborio or short-grain rice
Salt
Pepper from the mill
⅔ cup grated Parmesan cheese

1. Bring 2 quarts of water to a boil. Add salt and pepper. Place each vegetable in a strainer or colander inside the pot. First cook the peas for 4 minutes; lift the colander out and refresh under cold water. Use the same procedure for these other vegetables: the beans— 6 minutes; the carrots—6 minutes; the white radishes—7 minutes. Mix and set aside. Keep the water in which you cooked the vegetables.

2. Quarter the zucchini and yellow squash, and if the sticks are large, cut them up. Cut each piece of squash into ¾-inch chunks. Heat the 2 tablespoons of butter or oil in a skillet and sauté for 3 to 4 minutes. Salt and pepper. Add the other vegetables to the skillet. Set aside.

3. Have warm broth or vegetable cooking water ready on

the stove. Heat the ½ cup of butter or oil in a large saucepan or sauté pan. Add the onions and sauté until translucent. Add the rice and sauté in the butter until very hot.

4. Add enough broth (about one third of it) to cover the rice and let simmer until absorbed. Repeat the operation twice more, or until the rice has absorbed all the broth, is slightly mushy in appearance, and the rice grains are *al dente*.

5. Gently fold in the cooked vegetables. Add salt and pepper to taste. Serve with the cheeses.

RISOTTO WITH RADICCHIO

Serves 6

This dish is a specialty of the Hotel Due Torre in Verona. If you have no radicchio, do not hesitate to finely mince a head of escarole and use it exactly as described below.

    ½ cup butter or oil
    3 onions, very finely minced, about 1¼–1½ cups
    1½ cups Italian arborio or short-grain rice
  4½ to 6 cups warm, very light chicken broth or vegetable cooking water
    3 small heads radicchio, or 1 large escarole
    1 tablespoon butter
    1 cup heavy cream
    Salt and pepper
    ½ cup Parmesan cheese

1. Heat the ½ cup of butter or oil in a large saucepan or sauté pan. Add the onions and sauté until translucent. Add the rice and sauté in the butter until very hot to the tip of your finger.

2. Add enough broth to cover the rice and let simmer until absorbed. Repeat the operation twice more, or until the rice has absorbed all the broth, is slightly mushy in appearance, and the rice grains are *al dente*.

3. While the rice cooks, separate the leaves of the radicchio or escarole. Bring a large pot of water to a boil and parboil the leaves for 1 minute, no more. Drain and cool. Roll the leaves into cigars and cut into a chiffonade (thin strips).

4. Heat 1 tablespoon of the butter in a large skillet. Add the chiffonade and pour the cream over it. Cook down to ⅔ cup; salt and pepper well.

5. When the rice is cooked, blend the creamed radicchio into it. Serve promptly, sprinkled with Parmesan cheese.

COOKING GRAINS FOR PILAF

The pilaf method is well known to all, and whoever invented it can be considered a very smart person. Basically, the grain is cooked in fat before liquid is added. As result, a dry layer of overcooked starch builds around the grain kernels. This dry layer acts as a filter for the liquid used to cook the grain and prevents it from releasing starch on its outside. Each grain remains intact, and no stickiness develops in the mass of the cereal. This method works especially well with over-ripe rices, converted or not, and you can use any of the grains available in supermarkets, as well as the famous Basmati rice that tastes so pleasant.

In the following recipes, I use exclusively whole grains because they have more nutrition. Notice that the ratio of water to grain varies with each dish. One cup of large-grain polenta or corn grits will absorb 4 cups of liquid. One cup of rice, white or brown, will absorb 2 cups of liquid. One cup of bulgur will absorb 2 cups of liquid. One cup of barley will absorb 4 to 4½ cups of liquid, sometimes even 5. One cup of buckwheat groats will absorb 2 cups of water.

Pilafs can be prepared with diverse grains, but do not cook all the different grains together because each grain's cooking time varies. It is better to cook as many small pilafs as you have and mix them after cooking.

BARLEY AND MUSHROOM PILAF

Serves 6

Barley is the very best grain to cook with all types of mushrooms. Any forest mushroom you can find, from morels in the spring to late fall boleti, will do just fine. The ratio below is possible year round by mixing a blend of fresh commercial mushrooms and a few wild ones.

FOR THE MUSHROOM GARNISH
1 pound fresh mushrooms, cleaned
1 ounce dried mushrooms
2 tablespoons butter or oil
  Salt
  Pepper from the mill
1 clove of garlic, chopped
2 tablespoons parsley, chopped
1 cup heavy cream

FOR THE PILAF
½ cup butter or oil
3 medium onions, finely chopped
1½ cups barley
2 tablespoons each chopped chives and parsley

1. Slice the fresh mushrooms and soak the dried mushrooms in enough lukewarm water to cover comfortably.

2. Heat the 2 tablespoons of butter or oil in a large skillet. Add the sliced fresh mushrooms and sauté for a few minutes. Salt and pepper. Cover and let the juices run out of the mushrooms. Strain the juices into a bowl. Add to this bowl the soaking water of the dried mushrooms. Measure the total quantity and add enough water to make 6½ cups; heat and have ready. Chop the rehydrated mushrooms and add them to the pan containing the sliced mushrooms. Finish browning all the mushrooms together. Add garlic and parsley and heavy cream, and simmer until a saucelike texture results. Set aside.

3. *To cook the barley:* Heat the ½ cup of butter or oil in a large skillet and add the onions. Cook them until translucent. Add the barley and cook until the grains turn white. Add the heated mushroom water to the barley. Bring to a boil. Reduce and simmer for 20 to 25 minutes. Serve the barley topped with the reheated mushroom cream, and sprinkle with chopped parsley and chives.

BOURBON BULGUR PILAF

Serves 6

This pilaf can be served with the same mushroom or tomato garnish as in the recipes for Barley and Mushroom Pilaf (see page 77) and Corn Grits with Okra and Squashed Tomatoes (see page 69). You can, in this particular recipe, use your favorite bourbon. I use Jack Daniel's.

> ½ cup dried currants or raisins
> 1 tablespoon bourbon of your choice
> 5 tablespoons butter or oil
> 4 onions, finely chopped
> 1½ cups bulgur
> 3 cups light broth
> 1 cup very coarsely chopped pecans

1. Soak currants or raisins in bourbon. Set aside.

2. Heat 4 tablespoons of the butter and sauté the onions in it until they are translucent. Add the bulgur and toss well until hot to the tip of your finger. Add the broth. Bring to a boil, turn down to a simmer and cook on low heat, covered, for 20 to 25 minutes.

3. When ready, add the currants or raisins and their liquor; let stand for 10 minutes while you sauté the pecans in 1 tablespoon butter. Stir in the pecans.

BULGUR CUTLETS

Serves 6

These are wonderful for a nutritious vegetable main course. They consist of cooled bulgur pilaf mixed with cooked vegetables and beaten eggs and then shaped into cutlets, floured and fried in butter or oil the way regular meat cutlets are.

> 5 tablespoons butter or oil
> 2 small zucchini, diced into ⅛-inch cubes
> 2 shallots, chopped finely
> 6 mushrooms, finely diced
> ½ teaspoon finely crumbled dried basil
> 2 cups cooked bulgur wheat or other grain
> 2 eggs, well beaten
>   Salt
>   Pepper from the mill
> ⅓ cup flour

1. Heat 2 tablespoons of the butter or oil in a skillet and in it cook the zucchini, shallots, and mushrooms until all the juices have evaporated. Add the basil. Stir this mixture into the bulgur. Add the eggs and season to your taste with salt and pepper. Shape into 6 cutlets. Dredge in the flour. Heat the remaining 3 tablespoons of butter or oil and fry the cutlets until golden on both sides. Serve with plenty of green vegetables or a green salad.

WARM WEHANI RICE PILAF SALAD

Serves 6

This pilaf is an excellent meal in itself, served hot and sprinkled with loads of good grated cheese. Wehani is a brownish-red rice which has a delicious nutty taste reminiscent of pecans. It can be found in health food stores.

> **FOR THE PILAF**
> ¼ cup butter or oil
> 3 large onions, finely chopped
> 1½ cups wehani rice, or 1½ cups brown rice
> 3 to 3½ cups light broth

FOR THE SALAD
2 tablespoons olive oil
1 head escarole, finely chopped
1 dozen cherry tomatoes
1 pound mozzarella, slivered
½ cup slivered scallions

FOR THE DRESSING
Juice of 1 lemon
½ teaspoon salt, or more if needed
Pepper from the mill to taste
¼ cup virgin or light olive oil or other oil

1. Heat the butter in a large skillet, add the onions and sauté until translucent. Add the rice and toss until grains are well coated and heated through. Add the broth, cover and simmer.

2. Heat the 2 tablespoons of olive oil and in it stir-fry the escarole and the tomatoes for 1 minute. Fold the greens and tomatoes into the warm rice. Add the mozzarella until it starts to melt. Turn into a bowl and serve heavily sprinkled with slivered scallions.

3. Mix together lemon juice, salt, pepper and olive oil until you have a smooth dressing. Pass it in a bowl with the salad.

WATER FLUFFING OF WILD RICE

Wild rice is so good and so expensive that every step must be taken to guarantee that it will retain its glorious Northern Plains taste. The

**Fillet of Sole
with Provençal Flavors**
(p. 130)

**Grilled Salmon with
Smoked Salmon and Bacon Butter**
(p. 133)

Mussel Soup, Basque-Style
(p. 142)

**Lobster,
Papaya and
Avocado Salad**
(p. 104)

Dried apricots

**Glazed Duck Legs with
Apricot and Pistachio Couscous**
(p. 163)

**Panfried Breast of Duck
with Apples and Radicchio**
(p. 168)

best method I have found is to soak it in several successive baths of warm water, and then to cook it for a short period of time. One pound of rice will feed 8 to 10 people handsomely.

WILD RICE TIMBALES WITH TWO-GARLIC SAUCE

Serves 8

1 pound wild rice
2 tablespoons butter
2 onions, finely chopped
2 cups milk or half and half
8 eggs
Salt
Pepper from the mill
1 recipe Two-Garlic Sauce (see page 82)

1. Place the wild rice in a large bowl and cover with luke-warm water. Let soak for 1 hour. Drain. Repeat this procedure twice more, or until the grains become fluffy and open a bit. Drain thoroughly under cold water.

2. In a large saucepan, heat the butter over medium heat, add the onions and cook until translucent. Add rice, cover, and let steam for 10 minutes over medium low heat. (See Note.)

3. *To make the timbale:* Transfer the cooked rice to a large bowl. In another large bowl, beat the milk and eggs quite well. Add the rice and toss. Season with salt and pepper.

4. Butter 8 custard cups or ramekins and fill with the rice mixture. Place in a large metal baking dish. Fill the baking dish with boiling water halfway up. Bake in a preheated 325° oven for about 20 minutes, or until the custard has set. Remove custard cups from baking pan. Allow to cool slightly and then unmold onto a serving plate. Serve with Two-Garlic Sauce.

NOTE: If you wish to serve wild rice plain, season with salt and pepper after Step 2 and serve immediately.

TWO-GARLIC SAUCE

          4 tablespoons butter
         30 cloves garlic, peeled
          1 cup light cream
            Salt and pepper
          2 teaspoons cornstarch
          1 clove garlic, mashed
     2 to 3 tablespoons parsley, chopped

1. Melt the butter over medium low heat. Add the peeled garlic cloves. Cover and cook slowly for about 45 minutes, or until the garlic becomes completely soft. Check during cooking time to see that garlic does not burn. Lower heat, if necessary. Add the light cream and simmer, uncovered, for 5 to 6 minutes. Put in the blender and process to a smooth puree. Season to taste.

2. Stir the cornstarch into a small amount of the garlic puree in a small bowl. Bring the remainder of the garlic sauce to a boil. Turn down to a simmer. Add the cornstarch mixture, stirring constantly, and thicken on medium heat. Add the raw garlic clove and parsley and serve over the rice molds.

MODERN
SALADS

There was a time, not too long ago, when salad in this country meant iceberg lettuce and bottled salad dressing. But now there seems to be a salad revolution going on. Perhaps it was the salad bar that led to the uprising. All of a sudden, we could walk into a restaurant and find choices for salad ingredients that seemed to stretch far into the horizon. Supermarkets, Oriental grocery stores, even fast-food restaurants have joined the movement.

And the revolution has not stopped there. No longer does iceberg lettuce enjoy its monopoly over the salad bowl. Supermarkets and farmers' markets offer us a whole array of lettuces like red leaf, romaine, Boston, Bibb, arugula, chicory, endive and a brilliant red lettuce known as radicchio. Even the iceberg lettuce I get from Glen, my local farmer in the White Mountains in New Hampshire, doesn't look like the bowling ball we have known for so long. The iceberg he brings me is absolutely lovely, with wide, fresh outer leaves and a sweet and crisp middle. A lot of this interest in new salad greens began in California, where they have borrowed many of the concepts from the salads of Provence in the south of France. For example, Alice Waters, my friend at Chez Panisse, has popularized the idea of using baby lettuces, which make the most beautiful, tender, sweet salads you will ever eat.

By the way, if you want a good salad in Europe, go to Italy, not France. When it comes to feeding themselves simply and elegantly, I think the Italians are much smarter. They have retained that wonderful habit of having a few greens, just fresh from the garden, tossed in a very, very light oil and vinegar or lemon juice dressing. The salad is served after dinner and helps to lighten the stomach.

But, to return to the salad revolution, the salad bar is really very close to what in classic French cuisine is known as a "composed salad." These are main course salads and, in addition to using the wide array of greens available, they can be made with almost anything left over in the icebox. It might be a few shrimp, perhaps what's left of a rice dish you served the night before, perhaps a piece of chicken you have floating around. Any leftovers can be marinated in dressing for a few minutes and then arranged around your greens to make a very nutritious meal. But a word of warning: it is the dressing that you put over your salad that ultimately makes the meal healthy or not. If you decide to douse your salad with 3 or 4 tablespoons of dressing, forget about weight loss; but if you just lightly coat your salad ingredients with a teaspoon or two of dressing, then you really will be eating healthily. And another piece of advice: choose the right oil. Of course, olive oil is the most delicious, but there are several polyunsaturated oils that are also quite tasty. My favorite is sunflower oil because of its taste and because it keeps quite well. I like corn oil for the same reasons, as well as for the fact that it is one of the least expensive oils.

Yet another aspect of the salad revolution is the many new oils available on the market. You can find them in supermarkets, speciality food shops and health food stores. Along with beautiful green virgin olive oils, you will find walnut and hazelnut oil. You can even find avocado and pineapple oils. They are all superdelicious and ultra-expensive. If you decide to buy these oils, please blend them with less expensive ones. They have strong tastes and should not be used by themselves. If you cannot afford them, you can make similar ones yourself at home. Just combine your favorite polyunsaturated oil such as sunflower or corn with a few hazelnuts, walnuts or slices of avocado. Blend them well and let sit for a few minutes. The results won't be the same as the very expensive oils, but these oils will add a distinct accent to your salads. You can do the same with vinegars. Raspberry, tarragon, black currant, garlic and many other flavored vinegars are available in stores at rather high prices. Once again, you can make your own and end up with a very delicious one.

The recipes that follow are for some of my favorite salads. First are some simple salads to serve along with your meals; then come composed salads, which are divided into several categories: fruit, grain, high-protein (meats) and finally fish.

Before we begin, here are some tips on making delicious salads and dressings.

- Soak, then wash greens thoroughly in cold water.
- Remove the base or the rib of lettuce.
- Tear lettuce leaves into bite-size pieces, about 2½ inches square. Never use a knife—it will bruise the lettuce and cause it to discolor.
- Completely dry lettuce in paper towels or in a salad spinner (one of the great inventions of the twentieth century, as far as I'm concerned).
- Between one-eighth and one-fourth of the total volume of dressing should be an acid base such as vinegar or lemon juice. For 1 cup of dressing, there should be between 2 and 4 tablespoons of acid for ¾ cup oil.
- Always add salt, pepper, dried herbs or other seasonings to the vinegar and let sit for 15 seconds before adding oil.
- Whenever possible, use a blender to make your dressings. They will not separate as quickly as whisked or stirred dressings, and the flavoring will be more evenly dispersed.
- Use an egg yolk, 1 tablespoon of yogurt, heavy cream or sour cream, or 1 teaspoon of prepared mustard to stabilize (emulsify) dressings to keep them from separating and to add richness and body.
- When adding onion to salads or dressings, lightly salt it first and let it stand for several minutes to allow the strong juices to drain off; when using shallots, finely chop and squeeze them in a tea towel to remove the juice before adding.
- Rather than adding chopped garlic to a dressing, rub the salad bowl with a peeled, mashed head of garlic.

SIMPLE SALADS

The term "simple" comes from classic cuisine and refers to plain, tossed green salads. Simple salads are served with a meal, unlike "composed" salads, which are often a meal unto themselves.

CLASSIC GREEN SALAD

Serves 6

>   2 medium heads Boston lettuce
> 1 to 2 tablespoons red wine vinegar or lemon juice
>   ½ teaspoon salt
>   ¼ teaspoon freshly ground black pepper
> 6 to 7 tablespoons olive or corn oil or a mixture of the two

1. Carefully wash the lettuce. Remove center ribs or stems and dry the leaves thoroughly in a tea towel or paper towel.

2. In a blender container or a mixing bowl, combine the vinegar or lemon juice, salt and pepper. Blend or whisk well. Gradually add the oil and continue to blend or whisk until a temporary emulsion has been achieved. Toss the salad in dressing and serve at once.

SPINACH AND ASPARAGUS SALAD

Serves 6

This is a beautiful salad. Not only is there a difference in texture between the softness of the spinach and the light crunchiness of the asparagus, but the dark green spinach against the light green asparagus and the pale pink of the dressing makes a dazzling contrast for the eyes as well.

THE GREENS
½ pound fresh spinach leaves
12 warm asparagus, peeled and cooked to tender-crisp

THE DRESSING
18 fresh raspberries
1½ tablespoons raspberry or cider vinegar
⅓ teaspoon salt
½ teaspoon coarsely cracked black or white pepper to taste
4½ tablespoons corn oil or other polyunsaturated oil

1. Wash the spinach and remove the stems. Dry in a paper towel. Also dry the asparagus.

2. Put the raspberries, vinegar, salt and pepper in the blender and blend together well. Add oil and blend again.

3. Strain into a little bowl.

4. To assemble the salad, mix the asparagus and the spinach. Strain the dressing into the vegetables and toss rapidly together. Serve immediately.

ITALIAN BITTER-GREEN SALAD

Serves 6

This marvelous salad combines the bitterness of chicory with the sweetness of spinach leaves.

THE GREENS
1 head curly chicory, pale green leaves
3 Belgian endive
1 head radicchio
¼ pound spinach leaves

THE DRESSING
1 anchovy fillet, mashed
1 tablespoon lemon juice
3½ to 4 tablespoons virgin olive oil
Salt, if needed
Approximately ½ teaspoon coarsely cracked pepper

1. Wash the head of chicory and dry in a tea towel. Remove the core from the Belgian endive and cut each piece on the slant into slivers. Prepare the radicchio by removing all the old leaves around the head and then separating the other leaves from the centers. Wash them and roll them in a tea towel also. For the spinach, remove the stems, wash the leaves well and roll them in a tea towel. Before making the salad, combine all the greens.

2. *To make the dressing:* In a blender container, combine the anchovy, lemon juice, olive oil, salt and pepper and blend well. Just before eating, toss the salad and dressing and serve.

TOMATO SALAD WITH
WALNUT DRESSING

Serves 4 to 6

This is a tomato salad from the southwest of France. Be careful which tomatoes you use. The ones we get in the store nowadays are not always that good. The best are the sun-ripened tomatoes available from the end of July to the end of October. In the winter you may want to use those Holland or European tomatoes if you can find them. They taste almost like sun-ripened tomatoes. But do not ever refrigerate them. Year-round, you can use wonderful little cherry tomatoes, which can be so full of taste and so full of juice. Make sure you take the time and patience to let them get dark red on your kitchen counter or sunny windowsill.

THE GREENS
 1 pound ripest, best-tasting tomatoes you can find
18 leaves of arugula or chicory
18 chive flowers (optional)

THE DRESSING
 2 tablespoons red wine vinegar
 1 tablespoon armagnac or cognac
 1 pinch of sugar
 1 shallot, finely chopped and squeezed in the corner of a
   towel
 6 tablespoons walnut oil, or 6 tablespoons corn oil plus 6
   walnut halves
   Salt
   Coarsely cracked pepper, black or white, to taste

1. Blanch the tomatoes in boiling water; cool under cold running water and remove the skins. Slice the tomatoes. If they are cherry tomatoes, cut them in half. Wash and dry the arugula or chicory leaves. Keep the chive flowers refrigerated so they stay perky.

2. *To make the dressing:* In a blender container, mix the vinegar, armagnac or cognac, sugar, shallot, the walnut or corn oil and walnut halves, salt and pepper until well combined.

3. Neatly arrange the tomatoes on a large platter and surround them with the arugula or chicory leaves. Dot with the chive flowers. Pour the dressing over the tomatoes.

NOTE: Do not dress that salad ahead of time or the tomatoes will go limp. You may prepare the plate of tomatoes ahead; cover it with plastic wrap and keep it refrigerated until serving time.

VEGETABLE AND FRUIT SALADS

We do have a habit in America of eating a lot of fruit and putting it in the middle of our salads, and I think it is just about the best idea you can have. Salads with fruit are good for your health, and they have a wonderful texture, taste and look.

Choosing Fresh Fruit

Pay attention to the fruit you buy. The fruit in supermarkets has been put on a truck or train *before* it has had a chance to even develop its full sugar. You must ripen this fruit to make sure that it tastes good. Put it inside a brown paper bag. Close the paper bag and let it sit on the counter of your kitchen until the fruit is ripe. Check it about every half day. If you start with hard fruit, it will usually take three days to ripen pears, one to two days to ripen some peaches, nectarines and apricots. Berries do not ripen well in a paper bag; they tend to start molding at the bottom. So buy berries only when they are in season. (It's not really necessary to eat blueberries in February.) We have two crops of raspberries: the spring raspberries in June and July and another crop toward November, which comes from California.

PEAR AND BACON BITS SALAD

Serves 4

An unusual salad in which there are contrasts in tastes and textures.

FOR THE SALAD
- 4 slices bacon
- 2 tablespoons vinegar of your choice
- 3 pears, peeled and sliced
- 1 head romaine lettuce, washed, leaves separated and dried
- ¼ pound spinach leaves, washed, leaves separated and dried

FOR THE DRESSING

2 tablespoons grated Parmesan cheese
2 anchovies (optional)
½ tablespoon olive or polyunsaturated oil
Salt
Coarsely cracked pepper

1. Place the slices of bacon in a cold skillet and then cook slowly until crisp. Remove to a paper towel to drain. Crumble and set aside.

2. Discard the fat from the frying pan and add the vinegar, using it to dissolve any browned material in the pan very well.

3. Peel and core the pears, cut into ¼-inch slices, and toss the pear slices with the lemon juice. Set all these ingredients aside.

4. *To prepare the dressing:* Put the grated Parmesan, the anchovies, if desired, the vinegar, and the olive or polyunsaturated oil in a large bowl. Mix very, very well with a whisk or fork, add salt and pepper to taste. Add the romaine, spinach leaves and pears to the bowl. Toss together well, making sure the dressing coats all ingredients evenly. Serve the salad sprinkled with the crumbled bacon.

GREENS, FRUIT AND FLOWER SALAD

Serves 4 to 6

This salad is made with Meyer lemons, sweet-tasting lemons which are native to California. If you can't get them, regular lemons will do just fine.

FOR THE SALAD

¼ pound arugula, or 12 large leaves mustard greens
1 red leaf lettuce
3 oranges, peeled to the blood and cut into ⅛-inch slices
2 Meyer lemons, peeled to the blood and sliced (optional)
18 purple or orange nasturtium flowers (optional)

FOR THE DRESSING
Juice of 2 Meyer lemons, or 2 tablespoons lemon juice
plus 2 tablespoons orange juice
Salt
Pepper from the mill
½ teaspoon each grated lemon rind and grated orange rind

1. Clean and dry the arugula or mustard greens and the red leaf lettuce. Arrange on a plate and place the orange and lemon slices on top. Decorate all around with the nasturtium flowers.

2. *To make the dressing:* Put the lemon juice or lemon and orange juice, salt, pepper, grated lemon and orange rind into the blender container and blend until homogeneous. Just before serving, spoon the dressing over each portion of salad.

DANISH FRUIT AND CUCUMBER SALAD

Serves 6

Dieters can replace the cream in this dressing with low-fat yogurt.

FOR THE SALAD
1 head Bibb lettuce
½ pint fresh strawberries, sliced
½ pint fresh blueberries, preferably wild
18 raspberries
1 long European cucumber or 1 large cucumber, peeled, cut in half lengthwise, seeded and sliced in ¼-inch half-moons
1 tablespoon chopped shallots
1 bundle watercress, cleaned, in tiny bouquets

FOR THE DRESSING

⅓ cup sour cream

2 tablespoons light cream or milk

2 tablespoons raspberry vinegar, or 2 tablespoons cider vinegar plus 6 raspberries

½ teaspoon salt

Pepper from the mill

1. Clean, remove stems from, and dry lettuce leaves. Line a platter with them.

2. Arrange on top of a mixture of strawberries, blueberries, the raspberries, and cucumbers. Sprinkle with the chopped shallots. At the edge, here and there put some very bright leaves of watercress.

3. *To prepare the dressing:* In a blender container, blend all the dressing ingredients and homogenize well. Pour the dressing into a boat so that each guest can help himself to just the quantity he would like.

AVOCADO, CITRUS AND GREENS SALAD

Serves 4 to 6

A modern salad combining both sweet and sour ingredients with a sweet and sour dressing.

FOR THE SALAD

1 large red onion, peeled and sliced paper-thin
  A few grains salt
1 head kale or curly endive, cleaned and separated into
  leaves
2 navel oranges, peeled to the blood and cut crosswise into
  ¼-inch-thick slices
1 pink grapefruit, peeled to the blood and cut into ¼-inch-
  thick slices
2 avocados, peeled, pitted, each half cut into ¼-inch-thick
  half-moons

FOR THE DRESSING

2 tablespoons vinegar
1 tablespoon honey
  Salt
¼ teaspoon hot pepper flakes
4 tablespoons avocado oil, or corn oil plus 1 slice avocado

1. Sprinkle the onion slices well with salt and let stand for 10 to 15 minutes. Pat dry with a paper towel.

2. Line the edge of a plate with the leaves of kale or endive and fill the center with alternated slices of oranges, grapefruit, avocado, and onion.

3. *To make the dressing:* Blend all the dressing ingredients together. Just before serving, spoon the dressing over the fruit.

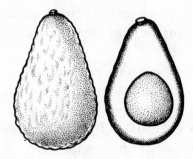

HIGH-PROTEIN GRAIN SALADS

These salads are for those of you who are vegetarians or who do not care to eat meat at lunch or even at dinner. There is nothing like a good grain to fill your stomach and keep you going on solid energy for a nice long time.

PROVENÇAL RICE SALAD

Serves 6

This is a lovely salad for a hot summer day.

FOR THE SALAD
3 cups cooked rice, white or brown
6 tomatoes, peeled, seeded and cubed in ⅓-inch pieces
2 zucchini, unpeeled, and cubed in ⅓-inch pieces
½ cup scallions, sliced in ⅛-inch slices
2 tablespoons pine or pignoli nuts or slivered almonds
12 large leaves of fresh basil

FOR THE DRESSING
2 anchovy fillets
¼ teaspoon dried oregano
¼ teaspoon dried thyme
⅓ cup basil leaves
¼ cup red wine vinegar
¾ cup olive oil or polyunsaturated oil
Salt, as needed
Coarsely cracked pepper
Parmesan cheese (optional)

1. In a large bowl, mix the rice, tomatoes, zucchini, scallions, and pine or pignoli nuts, and arrange the basil leaves around the edge of a large serving plate.

2. *To make the dressing:* Put the anchovy fillets and the herbs into a blender container, add the vinegar and oil, salt and pepper and process until it is very homogeneous.

3. Add the dressing to the rice and toss well. Place the rice on the serving plate and sprinkle with Parmesan if desired.

CHRISTMAS MIXED-GRAIN AND NUT SALAD

Serves 6

This is a delicious salad to serve in winter with holiday meals or at lunch by itself.

FOR THE SALAD
  1 cup cooked wehani rice, warm
1½ cups cooked coarse corn grits, warm
  1 cup cooked barley, warm
  ½ cup dark raisins
  ⅓ cup pistachios or almonds, peeled and coarsely chopped
  ½ cup coarsely chopped parsley

FOR THE DRESSING
     Juice of 1 lime
  2 tablespoons pomegranate or cranberry juice
     Juice of 2 cloves garlic
     Salt and pepper
  6 tablespoons avocado oil, or corn oil plus 1 slice avocado
 24 kumquats, cut into slices and seeded

1. Combine the wehani rice, corn grits and barley in a large bowl. Add the raisins, nuts and parsley.

2. *To make the dressing:* Combine the lime juice and pomegranate or cranberry juice, the garlic juice (obtained by pressing the cloves in a garlic press), the avocado oil, salt and pepper in a blender container and homogenize well. Pour the dressing over the grain mixture.

3. To serve, mound the grain on a plate and border it with the kumquat slices.

HIGH-PROTEIN MEAT SALADS

Meat salads are a delicious way to use leftovers that you have in your icebox. For example, at Easter, make a ham salad, at Thanksgiving or at Christmas a turkey salad.

HAM AND FRUIT SALAD

Serves 4

The fruit in this salad is there to temper the salt of the ham. If, however, the ham is much too salty for your taste buds or dangerous for your blood pressure, do not hesitate to soak it in milk for 2 hours to leach out the salt.

FOR THE SALAD
1 large ham steak, defatted and cut into ½-inch cubes
1 head Boston or 2 heads Bibb lettuce, cleaned
2 avocados, peeled and cubed
2 pears, peeled and cubed
1 tablespoon lemon juice
¼ cantaloupe, peeled and diced in ¼-inch cubes
3 oranges, peeled to the blood and sectioned
1 ripe pineapple, peeled, cored and cut into ½-inch tidbits

FOR THE DRESSING
1 tablespoon lemon juice
1 tablespoon white wine vinegar
1 tablespoon prepared horseradish
Salt to taste
Pepper from the mill
¼ cup slivered scallions, white and green parts
½ cup light cream

1. Soak the ham, if needed, to remove salt. Drain, dry and cut in pieces.

2. Roll the leaves of lettuce into large cigars and cut them across into a ⅙-inch chiffonade.

3. Line a 9-to-10-inch platter with the chiffonade of lettuce.

4. Combine the avocados and pears in a bowl and toss with the lemon juice. Add the cantaloupe, orange sections and pineapple chunks.

5. *To prepare the dressing:* Mix the lemon juice, wine vinegar, horseradish, salt and pepper in a blender container. Add the scallions and cream. Process in the blender until smooth. Let stand for 15 minutes and then strain into a bowl.

6. To assemble the salad, add the ham to the fruit mixture, toss well and mound it on the lettuce. Serve the dressing in a bowl.

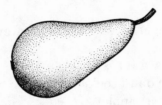

AIR-DRIED OR SMOKED MEAT AND MELON SALAD

Serves 4

In this salad, you may use any air-dried or cured meat you like: salami, prosciutto, Smithfield or Westphalian ham, or capicola.

FOR THE SALAD
12 slices of your favorite air-dried or cured meat, alone or in combination, rolled into small cornucopias
½ large cantaloupe, cut in ½-inch cubes
½ honeydew melon, cut in ½-inch cubes
1 slice watermelon, 1-inch thick, cut into ½-inch cubes
1 large cucumber, peeled, seeded and cut into ½-inch chunks

FOR THE DRESSING
¼ cup chopped mint
2 tablespoons finely chopped raisins
⅔ cup plain yogurt, full fat or low fat
Salt
Coarsely cracked pepper to taste

1. Arrange the cornucopias of dried meats around a 10-inch platter. Mix all the fruit and the cucumber in the center of the platter.

2. In a blender, combine all the dressing ingredients and serve in a bowl for guests to help themselves.

AUTUMN CHICKEN AND FRUIT SALAD

Serves 4

This is a wonderful way to use leftover chicken or turkey.

FOR THE SALAD
1 pound cooked, boneless white meat of chicken
2 tart apples, peeled, cored and cut into bite-size chunks
2 pears, peeled, cored and cut into bite-size chunks
Juice of 1 lemon
1 cup seedless grapes
2 ribs celery, washed and sliced slantwise in ¼-inch-thick slices
1 head Boston lettuce

FOR THE DRESSING
⅓ cup water
1½ teaspoons curry powder
½ cup mayonnaise, preferably homemade
1 teaspoon lemon juice
Salt and pepper
3 tablespoons chopped cilantro (fresh coriander) or parsley
¼ cup raisins

1. Cut the chicken into ½-inch cubes. In a large bowl, combine chicken, apples and pears and toss with the lemon juice. Mix with the grapes.

2. In a saucepan, blanch the celery in boiling water. Refresh under cold water. Add to fruit and chicken.

3. Wash and clean the lettuce. Remove the ribs and line a platter with the leaves.

4. Bring the ⅓ cup of water to a boil, add the curry. Cook for 1 minute and cool to warm.

5. Put the mayonnaise in a bowl. Add the lemon juice, salt, and pepper, and the curry water. Add the chopped cilantro. Toss the fruit and chicken mixture with the mayonnaise dressing and arrange over the lettuce leaves. Sprinkle with raisins.

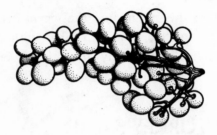

WARM CHICKEN OR DUCK LIVER SALAD

Serves 6

This is a delicious way to make non-liver-lovers love liver.

FOR THE SALAD
  1 head Bibb lettuce plus center leaves of one head romaine lettuce, washed, stems removed, and dried in a paper towel
  2 tablespoons corn oil
  3 duck or 6 chicken livers
  2 tablespoons Calvados, applejack, or cognac
  Salt and pepper

FOR THE DRESSING
  2 tablespoons cider vinegar
  ½ cup heavy cream
  Pepper from the mill

1. Crisp the lettuce leaves for several hours in the refrigerator.

2. Heat the oil in a pan. Add the livers. Cook them very quickly on each side, until they are resistant to the touch. The amount of cooking time depends on the size of the livers and on how well cooked you like them. Add the Calvados, salt and pepper. With a slotted spoon, remove the livers to a plate. Reserve any cooking juices in the pan. Keep warm.

3. *To prepare the dressing:* To the juices in the pan, add the cider vinegar and heavy cream. Cook for 1 minute to heat the sauce; cool to lukewarm.

4. Toss the greens into the warm dressing. Then place them on 6 small salad plates. Top each salad with one-half of a duck liver or 1 chicken liver, and freshly ground pepper. Serve immediately.

SMOKED TURKEY SALAD

Serves 6

Relatively new to the market, smoked turkey has a more opulent taste than plain turkey and offers a lot of good protein. In place of the smoked turkey you could substitute boiled ham.

FOR THE SALAD
¾ pound smoked turkey
1 head escarole, washed and dried in a tea towel
18 walnut halves, chopped
2 apples, peeled and sliced into ⅙-inch wedges
½ cup mild cheddar, cut into ⅙-inch slivers

FOR THE DRESSING
1½ tablespoons cider vinegar
1 tablespoon Dijon mustard with seeds
1 scallion, white part only, thinly sliced
Salt and pepper
3 tablespoons heavy cream
4½ tablespoons walnut or corn oil

1. Cut the turkey into bite-size pieces.

2. In a large bowl, toss together the turkey, escarole, walnuts, apples, and cheddar.

3. *To make the dressing:* Whisk the cider vinegar and seeded mustard with the scallion. Add salt and pepper, and whisk in the heavy cream and walnut or corn oil. Pour the dressing over salad. Toss well. Serve the salad on individual plates or on a large plate.

TURKEY, ORANGE AND KIWI SALAD WITH TEA AND SZECHUAN PEPPER DRESSING

Serves 4

Another way to use smoked turkey in a salad. This time, for summer. The unusual dressing is made with a Chinese tea available in supermarkets and specialty shops.

FOR THE SALAD
½ cup boiling water
1½ teaspoons Lapsang Souchong tea
12 small slices smoked turkey, 4 inches by 2 inches (about ¾ pound)
12 mustard green leaves, washed, trimmed and dried
3 oranges, peeled to the blood and cut in ¼-inch slices
4 kiwis, peeled and sliced on the slant into ¼-inch pieces

FOR THE DRESSING
2 tablespoons cider vinegar
1 teaspoon grated orange rind
½ small white onion
Salt
Pepper from the mill
6 tablespoons corn oil
1 teaspoon finely powdered, untoasted Szechuan pepper (optional)

1. In a small bowl, pour the boiling water over the tea and let steep for 10 minutes, covered.

2. Fold the slices of turkey into cornucopias and place a bunch of mustard greens into each. Arrange slices of orange alternating with slices of kiwi around the outsides of the serving plates. Garnish the plates with any leftover mustard greens.

3. *To make the dressing:* Mix the cider vinegar and orange rind. Grate the onion directly into the mixture. Add salt and pepper. Strain 3 tablespoons of the tea into the mixture, add the corn oil and homogenize well, with a whisk or in the blender. Correct the seasoning and pour over salad. Sprinkle the powdered Szechuan pepper on the salad.

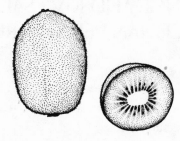

SHELLFISH AND FISH SALADS

Like adding meat to salads, including a little bit of fish for protein can make a healthy main course.

LOBSTER, PAPAYA AND AVOCADO SALAD

Serves 6

Who would have thought Maine lobster and tropical fruits would go together? Well, the same crazy cook combines vanilla, rum, garlic, and hot pepper flakes to make the dressing. Try it yourself to taste how wonderfully all these flavors come together. To make your own pineapple vinegar, soak the chopped core of one pineapple in 1 cup of white vinegar with 1 tablespoon of sugar for 5 to 6 hours.

FOR THE SALAD
2 lobsters of your choice, boiled
2 papayas, peeled
3 avocados, peeled
Juice of 2 limes
1 head red leaf lettuce, washed and separated into leaves

FOR THE DRESSING

  2 tablespoons pineapple vinegar
½ teaspoon honey
½ teaspoon hot red pepper flakes
    Salt to taste
1½ teaspoons pure vanilla extract
1½ tablespoons dark rum
  1 small clove garlic
  1 tablespoon heavy cream
  6 tablespoons corn oil
    Lime slices to garnish

1. Shell the lobsters. Cut the tails into ⅓-inch slices and each claw in half horizontally and lengthwise.

2. Cut the papayas and avocados in half, remove the seeds and pits. Cut crosswise into ⅓-inch slices and sprinkle the avocados with lime juice.

3. Mix the pineapple vinegar, honey, red pepper flakes, salt, vanilla, rum and garlic, and blend together very well in the blender. Add the cream and oil, and blend again. Correct the seasoning and strain into a small bowl. Place a bed of red lettuce leaves on a large plate and arrange pieces of lobster alternated with avocado and papaya slices over it. Pass the dressing in a bowl for people to help themselves.

NOTE: To turn this salad into an elegant meal for two, save the lobster shells and reassemble the lobster meat in them as shown in the photograph.

SHRIMP AND GREEN PEPPERCORN SALAD

Serves 6

Green peppercorns are available in cans or glass jars and can be found in some supermarkets and specialty food stores.

FOR THE SALAD

1 pound medium-size shrimp, cooked and shelled
1 medium red onion, chopped into ⅛-inch cubes
  Salt
  Pepper from the mill, in very small quantity
6 Boston lettuce leaves
2 cucumbers, peeled and seeded, cut into rounds ¼-inch thick
2 small zucchini, cut into rounds ¼-inch thick
2 small yellow squash, cut into rounds ¼-inch thick
2 tablespoons slivered scallions, green and white parts

FOR THE DRESSING

1 teaspoon grated lemon rind
2 tablespoons green peppercorns
3 tablespoons pineapple vinegar, (see page 104)
9 tablespoons corn oil
¼ cup chopped parsley

1. Cut the shrimp in half, lengthwise.

2. Sprinkle the red onion with a good pinch of salt and let stand for 15 minutes, if desired. Drain and discard juices.

3. Add the lemon rind, peppercorns and vinegar to a blender container and blend; add oil and blend well. Add the chopped parsley.

4. Line a platter with the Boston lettuce. In a bowl, toss the cucumbers, zucchini and squash with one-third of the dressing. Arrange in circular fashion over the lettuce leaves.

5. In the same bowl, toss the shrimp with the remainder of the dressing. Pile the shrimp in the center of the plate and sprinkle with scallions, and sprinkle onion on top.

WARM SCALLOP SALAD

Serves 4

This salad can be made with bay or sea scallops. Personally, I prefer sea scallops. I think they taste better and have a better texture.

½ pound fresh spinach leaves, washed and dried in a tea towel

FOR THE DRESSING
12 red currants or gooseberries, or 6 blanched cranberries
2 teaspoons lime juice
6 tablespoons corn oil
1 tablespoon heavy cream
Salt and pepper

TO FINISH THE SALAD
1 tablespoon corn oil
1 pound deep-sea scallops, washed and cut in ¼-inch pieces
Salt
Pepper from the mill
1 cup fresh red currants, gooseberries or blanched cranberries
Coarsely chopped parsley

1. Line a 10-inch platter with the spinach leaves; cover in plastic wrap. Set aside in the refrigerator.

2. *To make the dressing:* Put the red currants, gooseberries or cranberries and all other elements of the dressing into a blender, blend well and let stand for half an hour. Strain into a bowl, correct the seasoning, if necessary.

3. Heat the corn oil in a large skillet, stir-fry the scallops for 1 minute, salt and pepper them. Remove them from the heat for 2 minutes, and then pour into a colander placed over a bowl; let them drain. Add the scallop juices to the dressing and whisk briefly.

4. In a bowl, toss together the scallops and the berries and arrange them on the spinach.

5. Pour the dressing over the scallops and berries and sprinkle with parsley.

SALMON, ASPARAGUS AND DILL SALAD

Serves 6

This is an expensive salad and should be reserved for special occasions.

                6 ¼-inch-thick slices of fillet of fresh salmon, cooked
                6 slices of smoked Nova Scotia salmon (about ¼ pound)
                1 pound peeled, cooked asparagus, warm
                   Bouquet of dill sprigs
                ½ cup mayonnaise, preferably homemade
                ¼ cup reserved asparagus cooking liquid
        1 to 1½ tablespoons lemon juice
                   Salt
                   pepper from the mill
                ¼ cup chopped dill
                1 shallot, finely chopped and squeezed in the corner of a
                   towel

1. Alternate slices of cooked and smoked salmon in a circular pattern on the center of a plate. Arrange the asparagus and dill along the edges of the platter as decoration.

2. In a bowl, mix the mayonnaise, asparagus cooking water and lemon juice, salt, pepper, dill and shallot. Whisk well, and dribble over the salmon. Pass the remainder of the dressing to your guests in a little bowl.

FINNAN HADDIE AND POTATO SALAD

Serves 6

This salad idea comes halfway from Scotland, halfway from China. What a combination!

FOR THE SALAD
1 pound fillet of finnan haddie
1 quart milk
1 pound small red potatoes, peeled
Watercress bouquet
2 hard-boiled eggs
1 tablespoon parsley, chopped

FOR THE DRESSING
1 teaspoon dark soy sauce
2 tablespoons cider or rice vinegar
1½ teaspoons finely powdered, untoasted Szechuan pepper
6 tablespoons corn oil
¼ cup light cream

1. In a large pot, cover the finnan haddie with cold milk and bring to a boil. Turn off the heat, let stand for 7 to 8 minutes.

2. While the fish cools, boil the red potatoes in salted water. Simmer for 20 minutes or until tender when pierced by a knife. Keep them warm in the cooking water. Roughly chop the hard-boiled eggs.

3. *To make the dressing.* Blend the soy sauce, vinegar, Szechuan pepper, corn oil and cream in the blender.

4. Drain fish. Discard milk. Flake the fish and slice the potatoes while they are still warm. Mix them together in a bowl, add the dressing and toss well. Serve on the platter surrounded with the watercress. Top with the chopped egg and chopped parsley.

SMOKED TROUT AND BROCCOLI SALAD

Serves 6

This is a recipe for trout fishermen. Smoking your own fish is a lot easier than catching it.

FOR THE SALAD
½ pound spinach leaves washed and trimmed
6 smoked trout fillets, skinless and boneless
1 head broccoli flowerettes, peeled and cooked

FOR THE DRESSING
1 tablespoon cider vinegar
1 tablespoon Dijon mustard
⅔ cup medium cream
Salt
Pepper from the mill
⅓ cup toasted, chopped hazelnuts
2 tablespoons chopped parsley

1. Line a large platter with spinach leaves.

2. Arrange the trout fillets on the spinach and top each fillet with broccoli flowerettes.

3. *To make the dressing:* Whisk together the vinegar, Dijon mustard, cream, salt and pepper in a small bowl.

4. Spoon the dressing over the broccoli and trout fillets and sprinkle with the hazelnuts mixed with parsley.

FISH

Human nature will be human nature. In this country, and to a lesser extent in Europe, many people have relegated fish to secondary fare, to be eaten only as an occasional respite from meat. On Fridays, many of us learned to endure very overcooked fish served either under a rusty blanket of paprika or heavily breaded and deep-fried to resemble some form of aquatic French fry. Even what is now considered luxury fish often went unappreciated. Early colonial history has it that those poor indentured servants of New England had it specified in their work contract that they could be served salmon and lobster only twice weekly. And thick slabs of gorgeous swordfish served in school lunchrooms across America were left behind for peanut-butter-and-jelly sandwiches and slices of pizza.

Well, fortunately, human nature does change. Nowadays we have come to prize fish as being both delicious and healthy fare. Recent medical research has even suggested that by eating fish at least twice a week we can actually lower our cholesterol levels. And the new popularity of fish has been well documented. Seaports long decaying on the East Coast have been refurbished, not to sell fish in markets but to serve it to hungry customers in countless seafood restaurants. Perhaps most dramatically, the price of fish has soared. Only true market demand could motivate such inflated prices.

Fish has become so popular that the ocean supply is markedly dwindling, as none other than Jacques Cousteau himself warns. In response, human inventiveness has led us to find ways to raise fish in controlled environments from fertilized eggs—aqua farming. In Ossipee, New Hampshire, near my home in the White Mountains, an enterprising firm has undertaken raising Atlantic salmon. In a year's time the fish grow to between 1 and 2 pounds, and soon, when transferred to saltwater areas, these fish get as big as those born in their natural environment.

Fortunately, we in America are still blessed with somewhat fertile oceans. From the Georges Bank off New England, the bay waters of the Chesapeake, the Gulf of Mexico off Florida, Louisiana and Texas, and the watery expanses of the Pacific, we get a wide variety of fresh and delicious fish. And as our appetite for fish has increased, so too has an increased interest in how to cook fish developed.

I believe the Orientals, specifically the Japanese and the Chinese, have mastered the art of fish cookery. Most of the techniques that I now use and that are described in the recipes of this section have been adapted from Oriental techniques. While for so long the fashion was to overcook fish, cooks are now learning to leave the fish moist and succulent. No doubt the craze for sushi (the Japanese style of serving fish raw) has had a lot to do with this. A word of warning here: sushi must be made with absolutely fresh fish, and even then, the Japanese make sure to douse it with .wasabi, that pungent and purifying type of horseradish.

And while on the subject of trends in fish cookery, a word about fish sauces. In French we have a saying: *c'est la sauce qui fait le poisson,* which translates to "it is the sauce that makes the fish." Well, that was probably more true in the old days when an over-rich sauce was used to cover up the dried-out fish underneath it. Today, the trend is toward lighter fish sauces, and I am all for this. The sauce should not be so light that it floods to the bottom of the plate but, rather, should just coat the fish, leaving some evidence of the perfectly cooked flesh beneath it.

Here, then, are a series of recipes that incorporate Oriental and European techniques with our wonderful American fish. And may we together rejoice that human nature has changed and that fish has now become first-class eating.

VAPOR STEAMING

This method of cooking fish is done on a rack placed above boiling water in a pan so that the fish is kept isolated from the water. The pan is then covered, and as the steam rises, the fish is cooked. I particularly like this method because it is quick and easy and the texture of the cooked fish is incomparably moist, provided the fish is wrapped in a sheet of plastic wrap or a lettuce leaf to keep it from overdrying on its outside. The following two recipes are for vapor-steamed salmon, but halibut, turbot, lemon sole and red snapper fillets are also quite delicious cooked this way.

How to Form Medallions

1. Pass the blade of a small knife between the skin and the meat of a salmon steak and cut away the skin entirely. Discard it.

2. Remove the center bone gently with the same knife. You will have two pieces of salmon, a left-hand piece and a right-hand piece.

3. Leave the left-hand piece where it is and flip the right-hand piece over. To round the medallion, wrap the tail end around each center piece and secure with four toothpicks.

4. Place the thick part of the right-hand piece over the thin part of the left-hand one.

SALMON MEDALLIONS VAPOR STEAMED IN PLASTIC WRAP

Serves 6

6 steaks or medallions salmon, no more than ¾ inch thick
2 teaspoons freshly chopped dill
¾ teaspoon grated lemon rind

COMPOUND BUTTER

½ cup softened, unsalted butter
⅓ cup finely chopped dill weed
1½ teaspoons finely grated lemon rind
   Salt
   Freshly ground pepper

1. Season the salmon steaks lightly with a mixture of the chopped dill, lemon rind and a bit of salt and pepper.

2. Wrap each steak separately in plastic wrap.

3. Bring the water in the steamer container to a boil. Place the wrapped salmon packages on the steamer rack. Cover. Steam for 5 or 6 minutes for ¾-inch-thick salmon.

4. *To prepare the compound butter:* Combine the softened butter and the chopped dill weed, the grated lemon rind, salt and pepper to your taste. Cover the butter in plastic wrap and shape it into a roll, from which you can cut slices, or serve separately in small bowls. Refrigerate. Serve the medallions topped with a slice or a teaspoon of the compound butter.

SALMON MEDALLIONS VAPOR STEAMED IN LETTUCE LEAVES

Serves 6

6 salmon steaks or medallions
3 tablespoons chopped coriander and chervil
   Salt
   Freshly ground pepper
6 large leaves Boston lettuce, centers removed
⅔ cup fish stock (or fish fumet) or bottled clam juice
⅔ cup dry white wine
1 small shallot, finely chopped
½ bay leaf
1 tablespoon chopped parsley stems
   Pinch of dry thyme
⅓ cup reduced heavy cream (see Note)
   Lemon juice (optional)

1. Sprinkle the salmon steaks with 1 tablespoon of the coriander and chervil mixed together, salt and pepper. Wrap in the lettuce leaves.

2. Place the fish stock or fumet, wine and shallot, bay leaf, chopped parsley stems and thyme in the steamer container. Bring to a boil, turn down to a simmer. Put the wrapped salmon steaks in the steamer basket or on the steamer rack and steam for 5 minutes. Remove the steaks to a warm plate and cover tightly with a second plate. The salmon will finish cooking between the two plates while you make the sauce.

3. Reduce the steaming base to ½ cup. Add the reduced heavy cream and strain into a warm bowl in which you have put the remaining chopped coriander and chervil. Add a drop of lemon juice, if needed, and correct the seasoning with salt and pepper. To serve the salmon, open the lettuce leaves and spoon the sauce over the salmon within.

NOTE: To add heavy cream to a fish sauce, first reduce or cook down the cream by half its volume. You can prepare several cups at a time and keep it stored in the refrigerator, tightly sealed, to use when needed.

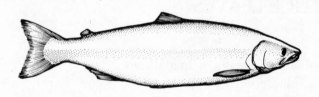

FOIL-STEAMED FISH

Whoever invented aluminum foil did us quite a favor, for it has proved to be wonderful as a disposable receptacle in which to cook. The foil does not let any moisture escape. The fish loses a bit of its juices into the packet, but these mingle with the vegetables there and add flavoring to form a sauce that is lean, delicious and accentuates the moistness of the fish flesh. Foil steaming is one of my favorite methods of preparing fish, not only because of the glorious taste and texture obtained but because it is neat and clean. Once you open that package and place its contents on a plate, there is no pot or pan to clean. If you wrap the fish securely, the jelly-roll pan on which you put the fish to bake will not even be dirty.

SALMON MEDALLIONS MAMIE SOLEIL

Serves 6

Mamie Soleil was a lady whom I knew when I was a little girl. A lot of other little girls knew her too, since she was a character in a book for young women who were just learning to cook and be good housekeepers.

>   6 salmon steaks or medallions
> 16 tablespoons chopped chervil or parsley
>   Salt
>   Freshly ground pepper
>   2 tablespoons noisette butter (see Note)
>   6 sun-ripened Italian plum tomatoes, peeled, seeded and coarsely chopped
>   2 tablespoons unsalted butter
>   6 squares of foil (9 × 9)

1. Season the salmon pieces with 2 tablespoons of the chopped chervil or parsley, salt and pepper, and set aside while you cook the tomatoes.

2. Heat the noisette butter. Add the tomatoes and cook for a few minutes until saucelike. Cool completely.

3. Preheat the oven to 400°. Butter six 9-by-9-inch squares of foil with the unsalted butter. Spoon half of the tomato mixture onto the bottom of each square of foil. Put one salmon medallion on top of each bit of tomato mixture and top with 2 tablespoons of the chervil or parsley and the rest of the tomato mixture. Wrap the foil securely by folding each end of the packet so no juices can escape.

4. Put the packets on a jelly-roll pan and bake for 10 minutes. To serve, open the foil packages and slide the baked fillets onto a warm plate. Garnish with the remaining 2 tablespoons of chopped chervil or parsley.

NOTE: "Noisette" literally means hazelnut. Noisette butter is used to give food a lovely, nutty, buttery flavor. To make it, melt butter slowly over a low flame and cook until it turns a dark russet brown. Make sure you don't cook it too quickly or it will suddenly turn black. Strain the butter before using.

SOUTHERN CALIFORNIA FOIL-STEAMED HALIBUT

Serves 6

This recipe evokes for me the fragrance of California citrus orchards.

    1   tablespoon unsalted butter
    6   halibut steaks, ¾ inch thick
        Salt
        Freshly ground pepper
  1½   teaspoons each lemon, orange and lime rinds, very finely
        grated
   ⅓   cup chopped coriander leaves

1. Grease six 9-by-9-inch squares of foil with the butter.

2. Salt and pepper the halibut steaks, sprinkle each with a good pinch of mixed lemon, lime and orange rind and 1 tablespoon of the chopped coriander leaves.

3. Put the packets on a jelly-roll pan and bake 10 minutes in preheated 400° oven.

4. Open the foil packages and pour the cooking juices of all into a small pan. Reduce the juices by one-third and add the remainder of the lemon, lime and orange rind mixture, coriander leaves and butter. Place the fish on a plate and spoon 1 tablespoon of sauce over each steak.

PAN STEAMING OF FISH

With this method, fuel use is minimal, since you start the fish in a cold skillet. Turn the heat on low. Once the flesh has whitened and become slightly firm, turn and repeat on the second side. Cooking the fish slowly in this manner lets the heat gradually penetrate to the middle of the fish, leaving it moist and succulent. For the last few minutes of cooking, place a lid on the fish and press down to force the heat into the center. You will know the fish is done when it feels resistant to the touch.

RED SNAPPER FILLET ESCABECHE

Serves 6

Escabeche is made in the Maghreb and in southern Italy with cooked fish and in Mexico as seviche, using raw fish and acidic marinade to cook the fish. The principle, passed on to us by the ancient Persians, is the same whether the fish is raw or cooked. The pleasures are great taste and a dish that can be prepared at least twenty-four hours ahead of time for company, with little fuss.

>   6 fillets of red snapper
>   7 tablespoons olive or corn oil
>   Salt
>   Freshly ground pepper
>   1½ tablespoons red wine or cider vinegar
>   1 small onion, very finely chopped
>   1 shallot, very finely chopped
>   1 clove garlic, mashed
>   ½ teaspoon freshly grated orange rind
>   ½ teaspoon freshly grated lemon rind
>   2 tablespoons parsley, coarsely chopped
>   1½ teaspoons paprika
>   ⅛ teaspoon cayenne pepper
>   Lemon slices
>   Italian parsley sprigs

1. Barely heat a skillet large enough to hold the fish fillets. Add 1 tablespoon of the oil, then the snapper fillets and cook them over very low heat until resistant to the touch. Put the lid on during the last 2 minutes of cooking to firm up the centers of the fillets.

2. While the fish cooks, put the remaining oil in the blender and add the salt, pepper, vinegar, onion, shallot, garlic, orange and lemon rind, parsley, paprika and cayenne. Blend well and correct the seasoning.

3. Pour one-half of the dressing into a glass baking dish. Add the warm fish and pour the remainder of the dressing over it. Cover the dish with plastic wrap and let marinate for 24 hours in the refrigerator.

4. Bring back to room temperature before serving. Place fillets on individual plates, spoon the marinade over them, and decorate with a lemon slice and some of the parsley sprigs.

CHILLED OCEAN PERCH OR SNAPPER FILLET ESCABECHE

Serves 6

This is an East Coast/West Coast version of the classic escabeche.

6 ocean perch or snapper fillets
7 tablespoons olive or corn oil
  Salt
  Freshly ground pepper
1 tablespoon lemon juice
  Grated rind of 1 lemon
3 tablespoons finely chopped coriander leaves or flat-leafed parsley, plus 6 whole leaves to garnish

1. Barely heat a skillet large enough to hold the fish fillets. Add 1 tablespoon of the oil and the perch or snapper. Cook the fillets over very low heat until resistant to the touch.

2. While the fish cools to warm, put the remaining oil in the blender, add salt, pepper, lemon juice, grated lemon rind and coriander leaves or parsley. Blend well. Correct seasoning.

3. Pour one-half of the dressing into a glass baking dish. Add the warm fish and pour the remaining dressing over it. Cover the dish with plastic wrap and marinate for 24 hours in the refrigerator.

4. Bring back to room temperature before serving. Place fillets on individual plates and garnish with coriander leaves or parsley.

MOUNTAIN TROUT FILLETS

Serves 6

All the wonderful trouts you can catch in the mountains during your vacations taste good. But the brown trout fillets are the treat of treats. Fillets from hatchery trout can also be used. The balsamic vinegar used in this recipe is a wonderful, somewhat sweet Italian vinegar made in the city of Modena. If you cannot find it, or find it too expensive, use standard cider vinegar.

> 12 fillets of brook trout
> 7 tablespoons corn oil, or 3 tablespoons corn oil mixed
> with 4 tablespoons hazelnut oil
> 1 tablespoon cider vinegar
> 1 tablespoon balsamic vinegar
> Salt
> Freshly ground pepper
> ¼ cup finely chopped chervil tops or parsley or coriander

1. Place the trout fillets in a large skillet with 1 tablespoon of oil and cook over very low heat until resistant to the touch. Put the lid on the skillet during last 2 minutes of cooking to firm up centers.

2. Blend the remaining oil with the balsamic vinegar, salt and pepper, and add the chopped chervil, parsley or coriander

3. Serve two fillets of trout per person and spoon an equal amount of dressing over each.

KING FISH AND EMPEROR WINE

Serves 6

Here is a luxury combination to be used for special celebrations. If French champagne is out of the question, any good California or French dry white wine will do very well.

FOR THE SAUCE

 1 cup good French champagne or California Chenin Blanc
 ½ cup bottled clam juice or fish fumet (see recipe opposite)
 2 shallots, chopped extremely finely
 1 teaspoon chopped parsley stems
 ½ bay leaf, crushed
 ½ teaspoon dried thyme
 12 tablespoons unsalted butter
 1 anchovy, mashed
 1 tablespoon chopped parsley
 6 lemon slices
 6 parsley bouquets

FOR THE FISH

 6 salmon medallions
 Salt
 Freshly ground pepper
 2 tablespoons butter

1. Mix the champagne or Chenin Blanc, clam juice or fish fumet, shallots, parsley stems, bay leaf and thyme in a small pot. Bring to a boil, turn down to a simmer and reduce until almost no liquid is left in the pan. Let the pan cool to warm.

2. Whisk in the butter, tablespoon by tablespoon, over very low heat. Add the mashed anchovy and strain the sauce into a boat. Add the parsley.

3. Melt the 2 tablespoons of butter in a large skillet, add the salmon medallions and pansteam over very low heat for 5 minutes, turning frequently. Cover with a tight-fitting lid and finish cooking for another 2 minutes.

4. Place each medallion on a plate with a slice of lemon and a bouquet of parsley. Spoon the sauce over the fish.

FISH FUMET (FISH BROTH)

Yields 5 to 6 cups

If you are lucky enough to have a fish market that can provide you with fish frames or skeletons you will be able to make your own broth. If not, use bottled clam juice. You can use any of the following fish frames for fumet: salmon, flounder, ocean perch, dab or snapper. Do not use frames from these fish, for they are too oily: mackerel, bluefish, striped or sea bass.

   Before you start, make sure you clean the fish bones thoroughly of any blood or traces of innards; the best way to do this is under cold, running water.

> 3 pounds fish frames (heads and bones)
> 2 onions, sliced
> 1 sprig fresh thyme, or 1 teaspoon dried leaves
> 1 bay leaf
> 2 dozen parsley stems
> 6 cups water
> 1½ cups dry white wine

1. Put all the ingredients into a large kettle. The water should just cover everything.

2. Bring the mixture to a boil and simmer for exactly 35 minutes.

3. Strain.

POACHING FISH

An efficient and fast way to cook fish is to immerse it in a boiling liquid. The liquid may simply be water (with 1½ teaspoons of salt), court bouillon, or even milk. Wrapping the fish either in plastic wrap or in a lettuce leaf prevents hardening of its outside.

A long, horizontal fish poacher fitted with a rack can be used, if you have one. Note that in all the recipes the liquid is brought to a boil, the fish to be poached is added, then the liquid is brought back to a boil, after which the heat is turned off immediately.

SALT-WATER-POACHED COD OR POLLACK STEAKS

Serves 6

Small trout, fillet of lake trout, fillet of pike can all be used in this recipe:

FOR THE FISH
6 cod or pollack steaks
Salt
Freshly ground pepper
2 tablespoons chopped parsley
1 small clove garlic, very finely mashed
6 large leaves Boston lettuce
1 tablespoon olive oil

FOR THE SAUCE
1 egg yolk
1 clove garlic, mashed
1 teaspoon finely grated orange rind
2 tablespoons basil, chopped to the point of being liquid
⅔ cup olive or corn oil
¼ cup poaching liquid

1. Season the cod or pollack steaks on both sides with salt and pepper and a mixture of the parsley and garlic. Wrap each piece of seasoned fish in a lettuce leaf.

2. Lightly grease the rack of the poacher with the tablespoon of oil. Place the fish packages on the rack.

3. Fill the poacher with 4 quarts of water and bring to a boil. Add 2 tablespoons of salt, add the rack with the steaks on top and immerse it in the rapidly boiling liquid. When the water returns to a boil, remove the poacher from the heat and let it stand, covered, for 7 minutes.

4. Meanwhile, mix the egg yolk, the garlic, the orange rind and the chopped basil, gradually adding the oil until a mayonnaise consistency is obtained. Add a small amount of the warm poaching liquid to lighten the sauce. Do not strain.

5. To serve, place each steak on a plate and open the lettuce leaf. Spoon sauce onto the leaf and over the fish.

POACHED SKATE WINGS WITH PINEAPPLE BUTTER

Serves 6

This is a true court bouillon poaching. Court bouillon is a classic seasoned poaching liquid made with water, wine, vinegar, chopped vegetables and a bouquet garni. The skate needs no protection during the cooking process due to its resilient texture.

FOR THE FISH
- 4 quarts water
- 2 cups cider vinegar
- 2 onions, coarsely chopped
- 1 large carrot, coarsely chopped
- 2 bay leaves
- 2 teaspoons thyme
- ¼ cup chopped parsley stems
- 2 tablespoons salt
- 1 tablespoon butter
- 6 skate wings

FOR THE SAUCE

1 cup chopped fresh pineapple
2 tablespoons pineapple or other vinegar
Salt
Freshly ground pepper
¼ cup strained court bouillon
2 tablespoons unsalted butter
4 tablespoons noisette butter
2 tablespoons chopped parsley

1. In the fish poacher, mix the water, vinegar, onions, carrot, bay leaves, thyme, and chopped parsley stems. Bring to a boil, add the salt and simmer for 20 minutes.

2. In another pan, cook the chopped pineapple with the pineapple vinegar, salt, pepper, and court bouillon for 10 minutes. Strain through a fine strainer. Bring the strained mixture to a boil, adding the unsalted butter, whisking very quickly. Continue whisking and add the noisette butter. Correct the seasoning with salt and pepper.

3. Lightly butter the rack of the poacher with the 1 tablespoon of butter and put the skate wings on the rack. Immerse them in the boiling butter-court bouillon mixture. As soon as the court bouillon comes back to a boil, remove the poacher from the heat, cover it and let it stand for 8 minutes.

4. To serve, pass a spatula between the skate meat and bone to separate the edible part. Put the meat on a plate or platter. Spoon the pineapple butter over them and sprinkle each portion with chopped parsley.

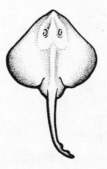

MILK-POACHED FINNAN HADDIE

Serves 6

The slightly salty taste of the fish is balanced by a lemony hazelnut-tasting butter.

FOR THE FISH
2 finnan haddie fillets
1 quart milk
Salt
Freshly ground pepper
1 teaspoon dried thyme
1 bay leaf

FOR THE SAUCE
⅓ cup noisette butter
2 tablespoons lemon juice
Salt
Freshly ground pepper
¼ cup chopped parsley

1. Place the fillets of finnan haddie in a pan. Pour the cold milk over them and slowly bring to a boil, adding a little bit of salt and pepper, the thyme and the bay leaf. Turn the heat off as soon as the milk comes to a boil and let stand, covered, for 5 minutes. Remove fillets and drain well.

2. Combine the noisette butter, lemon juice, salt and pepper and spoon over each portion of fish. Sprinkle with chopped parsley.

PANFRYING FISH

Nothing is easier or tastier than panfrying fish. This is not for people who are watching their cholesterol.

PANFRIED ITALIAN SARDINES

Serves 6

This dish is utterly delicious. The smell of the sardines will permeate the house, but is commensurate with the good taste.

      12 large fresh sardines, cleaned and patted dry
      ⅓ cup flour
         Salt
         Freshly ground pepper
       4 tablespoons clarified butter or olive oil
       1 lemon, cut in wedges

1. Coat the sardines well with flour seasoned with the salt and pepper.

2. In a frying pan, heat the butter or oil to very hot and fry the fish in it for 2 to 3 minutes on each side, until the skin is nice and crisp.

3. Serve each portion with lemon wedges.

MERLUZZO ITALIANO

Serves 6

      12 small whiting fillets
       3 tablespoons flour
      ½ cup fresh breadcrumbs
       1 clove garlic, mashed
       3 tablespoons parsley, finely chopped
       2 tablespoons Pecorino or Romano cheese, finely grated
       1 egg
       1 teaspoon and ⅓ cup corn oil
       1 teaspoon water
         Salt and pepper
       6 lemon wedges
       6 parsley sprigs

1. Flour the fillets of whiting.

2. Mix the breadcrumbs, garlic, parsley and cheese. Spread the crumbs onto a piece of wax paper.

3. Mix the egg, 1 teaspoon oil, water, salt and pepper and with a fork beat well to obtain a very homogeneous egg wash. Brush the egg wash onto one side of each fillet.

4. Invert the egg-coated side of each fillet into the crumb mixture. Brush the second side of each fillet with more egg wash and turn over again into the crumbs to coat the second side.

5. Pat smartly in your hand to remove any excess crumbs. Let dry for a few minutes.

6. Heat ⅓ cup of oil until it ripples and then quickly fry the fillets on each side until golden.

7. Drain on paper towels. Serve two fish per person with lemon wedges and parsley sprigs.

FILLET OF TROUT WITH BACON

Serves 6

If you live near an Italian market and you can find pancetta, an Italian pepper-cured bacon, the lightly crusted trout will take on a delicious Italian flavor.

12 trout fillets
2 tablespoons and ½ cup flour
Salt
Freshly ground pepper
1 egg yolk
1⅓ cups milk
2 slices of thickly sliced bacon or pancetta, diced
2 tablespoons chopped parsley
1 clove garlic, finely chopped
2 tablespoons oil

1. Coat the trout fillets with the 2 tablespoons of flour seasoned with salt and pepper.

2. Mix the ½ cup of flour with the egg yolk and turn into a shallow bowl. Blend in milk. Set aside.

3. Put the diced bacon or pancetta into a frying pan, fry until golden. Add the chopped parsley and garlic. With a slotted spoon, remove the mixture to a small bowl.

4. In the same pan add the oil. Dip each fillet into the flour mixture and fry over medium high heat until golden on both sides. Serve 2 fillets per person. Dot with the bacon, garlic and parsley mixture.

OVEN-BAKED FISH

This is an old-fashioned method of cooking fish. It's quite nice for a small dinner party.

FILLET OF SOLE WITH PROVENÇAL FLAVORS

Serves 6

> 3 tablespoons and ½ cup butter
> ½ pound sliced mushrooms
> Salt
> Freshly ground pepper
> 1 teaspoon orange rind, finely grated
> ¼ teaspoon lemon rind, finely grated
> 1 teaspoon powdered dry basil
> 6 large sole fillets
> ½ cup fish fumet (page 123), or bottled clam juice
> ¼ cup dry white wine
> ¼ cup heavy cream
> ⅛ teaspoon powdered saffron
> 1½ tablespoons slivered orange and lime rind, blanched

1. Heat 1 tablespoon of the butter in a skillet. Add the mushrooms and sauté them. Salt and pepper them, cover the pan and let the juices escape. Cool completely.

2. Butter a baking dish with 2 tablespoons of butter. Add the mushrooms, the grated orange and lemon rind and the basil and arrange the sole fillets on top. Mix the fish fumet or clam juice with the white wine and pour over the fillets. Cover the fillets with a sheet of parchment paper. Bake in a preheated 375° oven for 8 minutes. Remove the fish from the oven. Keep the fillets warm between two plates so they finish cooking while you make your sauce.

3. Drain the cooking juices and mushrooms from the baking pan into a skillet. Bring the sauce to a boil. Add the cream, then the ½ cup of butter. Correct the seasoning. Add the saffron.

4. Serve the fillets on a bed of the mushroom sauce and top with a mixture of the blanched slivers of orange and lime rinds.

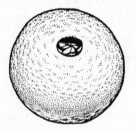

BAKED STRIPED BASS WITH SORREL HOLLANDAISE

Serves 6

Sorrel is a lemony-tasting herb also known as sour grass, available in some supermarkets in the late spring and early summer. Try growing it yourself; it grows easily. The tangy taste of the sorrel hollandaise brings out the delicate flavor of our wonderful native striped bass.

FOR THE FISH
1 large striped bass
5 pounds kosher salt

FOR THE SAUCE

½ cup water
1 tablespoon lemon juice
 Salt
 Freshly ground pepper
2 egg yolks
¾ to 1 cup melted, unsalted butter
 Salted water as needed
3 tablespoons finely chopped sorrel
 Parsley bouquets
 Lemon wedges

1. Place one-third of the kosher salt in a large baking dish. Add the bass, cover with the remainder of the salt. Bake in a preheated 375° oven for 35 to 40 minutes.

2. In a saucepan, mix the water, lemon juice and a pinch of salt and pepper and reduce to about 2 tablespoons. Cool the sauce slightly over low heat. Add the egg yolks, one at a time. Whisk as soon as each yolk is added to the pan and continue whisking until the mixture turns very white and extremely foamy. Gradually dribble in the melted butter, whisking strongly until all the butter is absorbed. Add salted water if necessary to thin the sauce to the texture of heavy cream. Add the sorrel and blend well. Correct the seasoning. The sauce will lighten even further when you add the sorrel, for it releases its juices into the sauce.

3. When the fish is done, spoon the salt out of the baking dish. Skin the fish and remove the top fillet to a platter. Lift out the backbone. Discard it and lift out the second fillet. Place it on the platter. Serve the fish with the sorrel hollandaise and decorate the platter with parsley and lemon wedges.

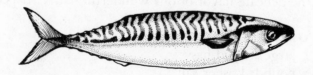

GRILLED FISH

Firm-fleshed fish such as salmon and swordfish can be grilled, with delicious results, either indoors or outside on the barbecue. Be sure to do one thing before you grill the fish: brush the grill and fish liberally with oil.

GRILLED SALMON WITH SMOKED SALMON AND BACON BUTTER

Serves 6

> 4 tablespoons unsalted butter, softened
> 1 teaspoon lemon juice
> ⅛ pound smoked salmon, finely chopped
> 2 tablespoons crumbled cooked bacon
> 6 salmon steaks or medallions
>   Oil for brushing grill and fish

1. Make compound butter: In a medium bowl, combine butter, lemon juice, smoked salmon and bacon bits. Stir together until well mixed. Place on a sheet of plastic wrap and roll into sausage shape. Refrigerate until ready to serve.

2. Heat grill over medium high heat.

3. Brush grill and salmon steaks with oil.

4. Place salmon steaks on grill and sear well on each side for about 3 minutes.

5. Turn down heat and continue cooking fish for another 2 to 3 minutes or until firm to the touch. Serve each medallion with a thin slice of the smoked-salmon and bacon butter. (Freeze any leftover butter for future use.)

GRILLED SWORDFISH WITH GORGONZOLA BUTTER

Serves 6

> 4 tablespoons unsalted butter, softened
> 1 teaspoon lemon juice
> 2 tablespoons Gorgonzola cheese, crumbled
> Dash of white pepper
> 2 tablespoons thinly sliced scallions, green part only
> 6 swordfish steaks
> Oil for brushing grill and fish

1. Make compound butter: In a medium bowl, combine butter, lemon juice, cheese, pepper and scallion greens. Stir together until well-mixed. Place on a sheet of plastic wrap and roll into a sausage shape. Refrigerate until ready to serve.

2. Heat grill over medium-high heat, and brush grill and fish with oil.

3. Place swordfish steaks on grill and sear well on each side for about 3 minutes. Turn down heat and continue cooking fish for another 4 to 5 minutes, or until firm to the touch. Serve each swordfish steak with a thin slice of Gorgonzola butter. (Freeze any leftover butter for future use.)

SHELLFISH

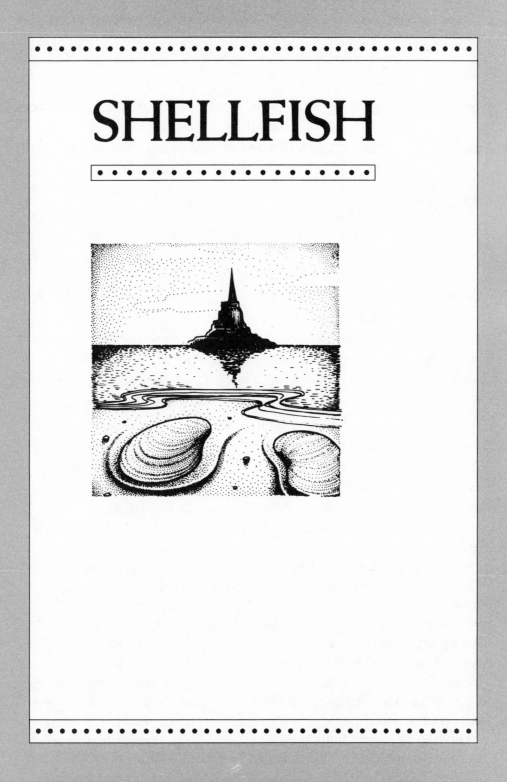

I have enjoyed the Atlantic seashore from the Gulf of Gascony to the tip of Brittany as well as the Mediterranean. I really thought I had seen all kinds of shellfish. But I was not quite prepared for what happened to me in Bar Harbor, Maine. The only thing I could say was "Wow, oh wow!" Wow, indeed. I went there as the lobster boats were coming in. I was accompanied by my husband, Alan B.; my 4-year-old son, Alan D.; our black Labrador, Whiskey; and my younger son, Neil, whom I carried on my left hip. My youngest was sitting there, contented, when all of a sudden he nearly escaped me, letting out the biggest wail, while the dog started to bark, retreated and whimpered, and nearly fell off the wall. The lobstermen were emptying their catch, and before us were the hugest, most beautiful American lobsters I had ever seen in my life. Some were a foot and a half long, some dark green, some bluish, tangled with seaweed. It relieved something in my cook's soul; I simply could not believe it. It was so beautiful, it even beat the unloading of salmon I had seen the year before at La Push, Washington, on the Pacific.

Sure enough, I bought a big 3½-pounder, brought it back to our little rented summer house, and as soon as young Neil had gotten over his lobster fright and he and young Alan had fallen asleep, exhausted by their first meeting with a lobster, Alan and I proceeded to cook the monster. The summer cottage had no appropriate vessel, so we sanitized Neil's metal baby bathtub, which accompanied us on all family trips, and cooked the lobster in it. I shoved in the tail, which was 2¼ inches wide at its thickest part (the big claws were 3 inches long). One would think that such a big thing would be tough. No way. It was succulent, full of good briny juice, and we both pigged out. We enjoyed it plain, as it was made: no butter, no clam broth, no steamy broth. Just a huge portion of one of the greatest luxuries the

American table has to offer. There was so much meat there that I made a salad with the head and small legs and found another bonus in the form of a bowl of eggs that had turned part burgundy, part bright red during the cooking. If you ever find such a bonus in a big lobster, do not throw it away. Not only is it good for you, but it tastes delicious in soups and sauces.

The next day I went down to the rocks, picked mussels, steamed them open, and with their juice, water, and the leftover lobster coral, made a great pot of soup that I thickened with a little cornmeal. It was a feast. A funny memory about that soup involves a gaunt gentleman who came to tell me something that back in 1967 was probably important. "Well," he said, watching me pick mussels, kind of dangling from one foot, then the other, "we don't eat those." I looked at him and I said, "Well, I do." Incredulously, he repeated it, as if I were too crazy to understand that the abominable mussel would do harm to me: "We don't eat those." I smiled at him again and repeated, "Yes, I know, but I do." We parted ways and exchanged no other words, and he was probably as disgusted with me for picking the mussels as I was annoyed at him for ignoring them.

Since that time, I have happily cooked with the abundance of America's wide range of shellfish. Over the past twenty-five years I have crossed the country many times, teaching. At each stop I've looked in the supermarkets and at fishmongers to see what shellfish was available locally. In the recipes that follow, you will find shellfish available only in certain parts of the country, such as the Olympia oysters of the Northwest, Maryland crabs, and Louisiana crawfish. Nowadays, with modern transportation, many regional items are available in big cities. Choose recipes in this section according to what you can find in your particular area. Be adventurous when you shop and ask your fish man to get you shellfish not readily available.

SCALLOPS

There are many types of scallops all over the world, and their shells come in many of the most dazzling colors. In the United States we generally divide scallops into two types: bay scallops and deep-sea scallops. Bay scallops are small, the biggest being as large as my thumb. In the Northeast we love the Cape Cod scallops, which are in season starting in mid-February. Be careful not to confuse them with the slightly smaller scallops of the southeastern Atlantic waters. The texture, taste, especially the sweetness of the northern scallops are far superior to those of the southern ones. The southern is best used as a garnish in fish or shellfish soup.

Generally, 1 pound of scallops serves 4–6 persons as a main course, 6–8 persons easily as a first course. If you serve big men with big appetites, use 1½ pounds of shellfish. Watch it, though. Everything is so very rich.

Stir-Frying Scallops

This method comes from Chinese cuisine and is definitely my favorite for scallops. By limiting the cooking to literally a few seconds, you will find that the scallops become utterly succulent, with a buttery tenderness.

STIR-FRIED BAY SCALLOPS WITH PISTACHIOS

Serves 4 to 6

This recipe is done in a matter of minutes. The only time-consuming part is peeling the pistachios. If you do not have the time, replace them with almonds, and substitute cognac for the kirschwasser.

1 pound bay scallops
2 tablespoons butter
Salt
¼ cup clam juice
¼ cup dry white wine
1½ teaspoons cornstarch
¾ cup light cream
1 teaspoon kirschwasser
3 tablespoons peeled, coarsely chopped pistachios

1. Clean the bay scallops. Set aside.

2. Heat the butter in a large skillet until it turns light brown. Add the scallops and stir-fry for 1 minute, salt them lightly, then remove them to a colander placed over a bowl to collect any juices.

3. To the skillet, add the clam juice, the white wine, and the reserved scallop juices. Reduce to 2 to 3 tablespoons and keep at a low simmer for a few minutes.

4. Mix the cornstarch with the light cream. Add to the skillet and thicken over medium heat. Turn off the heat and add the kirschwasser (or cognac, if you are substituting almonds for the pistachios).

5. Put the scallops in a serving dish. Strain the sauce over them and sprinkle with the pistachios (or almonds) and the coarsely cracked pepper. Serve immediately.

STIR-FRIED DEEP-SEA SCALLOPS WITH CHAMPAGNE SAUCE

Serves 4 to 6

This is a good dish to serve when entertaining. If the champagne and smoked salmon are too expensive, use a good plain dry white wine and skip the smoked salmon.

1 pound large deep-sea scallops, cut into ¼-inch slices
⅛ pound smoked salmon, diced

FOR THE SAUCE
  1 cup of champagne brut, preferably French
  1 cup fish fumet (page 123), or bottled clam juice
  3 shallots, chopped finely
  2 tablespoons chopped parsley stems
  ½ bay leaf, crumbled
  ⅛ teaspoon dried thyme leaves
  1 cup heavy cream
  ½ cup and 2 tablespoons unsalted butter

1. First make the sauce: Put the champagne, the fish fumet or clam juice, the shallots, parsley stems, bay leaf, and thyme in a medium-size saucepot. Reduce to ½ cup. Blend in the cream and reduce to 1 cup. Bring to a high boil and whisk in the ½ cup of butter, tablespoon by tablespoon.

2. Heat the remaining 2 tablespoons of butter in a skillet, and add the scallops. Stir-fry them for 2 minutes. Remove them to a colander placed over a bowl. Add the scallop juices to the sauce. Keep warm.

3. Blend the scallops into the sauce, reheat well, and at the last minute add the smoked salmon. Serve very quickly.

MUSSELS

The following recipes can be used for littleneck or cherrystone clams as well as for mussels.

STEAMED MUSSELS MARINIÈRE

Serves 4 to 6

  3 quarts mussels
  ½ cup dry white wine
  1 finely chopped onion
  2 finely chopped shallots
  2 tablespoons chopped parsley stems
  1 teaspoon coarsely cracked pepper

1. Scrub the mussel or clam shells thoroughly with a stiff brush or pot scrubber.

2. Place all the ingredients in a large pot with handles. Cover the pot, place over medium-high heat, and cook for 8 to 10 minutes. When the liquid boils, grab the pot by both handles (use potholders) and shake from time to time so that the shellfish will cook evenly.

3. After 8 minutes, remove all opened shellfish, cover the pot again and continue to cook remaining shellfish for another minute or two. Discard any that have not opened. They are not fresh and are inedible.

4. Serve in bowls with the strained cooking liquid and a large chunk of crusty French bread.

STEAMED MUSSELS WITH SAFFRON AND COGNAC SAUCE

Serves 4 to 6

This is an elegant variation of Mussels Marinière.

    1 recipe Steamed Mussels Marinière, above
1½ tablespoons cornstarch
    1 cup light cream
    3 tablespoons chopped parsley
    1 large pinch of saffron threads
    2 tablespoons cognac or other brandy

1. Reserve the mussels and the sauce marinière.

2. Put the cornstarch in a saucepan and gradually whisk in the light cream; thicken over medium heat. Set the thickened cream aside and keep warm.

3. Remove the empty half-shells from the mussels and pile the half-shells that contain the mussels into a bowl. Strain enough of the hot mussel juices into the cream to obtain a sauce that barely coats the back of a spoon. Strain it into a pot. Add the parsley, saffron threads, and cognac to the sauce. Reheat it well but without boiling it, and pour it over the mussels.

MUSSEL SOUP, BASQUE-STYLE

Serves 4 to 6

Very popular in the French villages of the Basque country, which borders on Gascony, this recipe probably has one hundred variations.

    2   tablespoons butter or corn oil
    2   onions, finely chopped
    3   cloves garlic, finely chopped
 1½   pounds sun-ripened tomatoes, peeled, seeded and
        coarsely chopped
    2   cups water
    1   teaspoon dried thyme
   ½   cup cornmeal
    1   cup dry white wine
    1   recipe Steamed Mussels Marinière (see page 140)
   ¼   to ½ teaspoon finely crumbled hot pepper flakes
    1   red pepper
    1   green pepper
    1   yellow pepper

1. Heat the butter or corn oil in a large pot. Add the onions and garlic, brown well. Add the tomatoes and mix well. Into the aromatics put the water and dried thyme, and simmer for 20 minutes.

2. Mix the cornmeal and wine, stir into the tomato base and let simmer for 10 minutes: add the reserved cooking juices from the steamed mussels marinière. Shell the mussels, add them to the liquid, reheat well and add the hot pepper. Mix well and let stand.

3. Seed and dice all the peppers. Sauté them in a dash of oil and add them to the soup as a garnish.

CLAMS AND OYSTERS ON THE HALF-SHELL

My favorite clam on the half-shell is the littleneck clam. I think the oysters grown in the Pacific Northwest, together with the Belon now grown in Maine, are the best. They are strongly reminiscent of the Fines-de-Clair of France, on which I was fed for five long war years: nice and briny with a frank, appetizing color. The Pacific Northwest has the beauty of beauties in America, that extraordinary little Olympia, which is between the size of a quarter and that of a silver dollar and which, as far as I am concerned, makes a quintessential oyster stew. Here are a few recipes to practice on.

GRILLED LITTLENECKS ON THE HALF-SHELL

Serves 4 to 6

36 littleneck clams
2 tablespoons finely diced ginger, blanched in boiling water
2 tablespoons finely chopped scallion greens
Salt
Pepper from the mill
1 tablespoon Worcestershire sauce
½ cup butter
⅓ cup heavy cream
Kosher or coarse salt as needed

1. Open the littlenecks, making sure that you pass your knife blade under each clam to sever its muscle and make the clam easy to remove from the shell at the table.

2. Put the ginger, scallion greens, salt and pepper to your taste, Worcestershire sauce and butter in a food processor. Cream together well and gradually add the heavy cream. Correct the seasoning. Put a small teaspoon of the mixture on top of each raw clam.

3. Sprinkle a ¼-inch-thick layer of kosher salt onto a large jelly-roll pan, set the clams on it and broil them for a few minutes, or until golden. Serve piping hot with crusty bread.

OYSTERS ON THE HALF-SHELL

Serves 4 to 6

The condiment used here is a variation of the well-known French *mignonnette*.

  2 tablespoons sherry vinegar or red wine vinegar
  2 tablespoons balsamic vinegar
  1 tablespoon Worcestershire sauce
  ½ cup dry white wine
  2 shallots, or 4 scallions, white part only, very finely
    chopped
    Salt
    Pepper from the mill
 36 oysters (any type you like or can find), in their shell and
    open

1. Mix the sherry vinegar, balsamic vinegar, Worcestershire sauce, white wine, shallots or scallions, salt and pepper to your taste and let sit covered, at least two hours.

2. Shell the oysters and keep them on the half-shell well refrigerated until serving. Before serving, sever the underside of the foot muscle so your guests can eat the oysters without struggling.

3. Serve the oysters with a tiny container of the prepared condiment for each guest, so he or she can put a few drops on each shellfish. Accompany the oysters with very good rye bread.

Oatmeal and Fresh Fruit
(p. 65)

**Spaetzle with
Cucumbers and Radishes**
(p. 173)

**Leek, Goat Cheese
and Walnut Pizza**
(p. 182)

**Berry
Napoleon
with
Lemon
Curd**
(p. 197)

Red, yellow and purple plums

Zwetschkekuche

(p. 186)

Lemon Blueberry Pie
(p. 190)

GRILLED OYSTERS WITH ENDIVE CREAM

Serves 6

If Belgian endive are not available to you, simply use the pale yellow center leaves of 1 escarole and 1 curly chicory. This recipe is best prepared with Maine Belon oysters.

> 6 small Belgian endive
> 2 tablespoons butter
> ½ cup fish fumet (page 123), or bottled clam juice
> 36 oysters
>   Salt
>   Pepper from the mill
> 1 cup heavy cream

1. Remove the stems from the endive. Wash the leaves quickly under cold running water. Pat them dry in a tea towel and slice them crosswise into shreds.

2. Heat the butter in a small pot. Add the endive shreds and cook them for about 20 minutes or until they are completely soft. Turn the heat off.

3. Shuck the oysters and strain their liquor onto the endive. Add the fish fumet or clam sauce and recook together for 10 to 15 minutes, or until the mixture has thickened. Add salt, pepper and cream and let simmer together for another 10 minutes. Pour into the blender and puree well.

4. Wash the oyster shells well in hot water; dry well.

5. Put a teaspoon of endive sauce at the bottom of each shell. Add the oysters and top each with another ½ to ⅔ teaspoon of cream and broil for 2 to 3 minutes. Serve as soon as the cream turns golden brown.

OLYMPIA OYSTERS WITH VINEGARED RADISH

Serves 6

A dainty little dish as a first course.

    1 cup sliced red radishes
    2 tablespoons butter
 1½ tablespoons cider vinegar
    Salt
    Pepper from the mill
  ½ cup heavy cream
   72 Olympia oysters
    3 tablespoons chopped Italian parsley

1. Sauté the radish slices in the hot butter. Add the cider vinegar and a pinch of salt and pepper. The radishes will turn bright red.

2. Add the cream and simmer for 2 to 3 minutes. Set aside.

3. Shuck the oysters and drop them and their liquor into a bowl.

4. Reheat the radish cream to the boiling point. Turn the heat off. Blend in the oysters and mix gently by shaking the pan back and forth. Add the parsley and correct the seasoning. It is essential that the oysters heat through but do not cook.

5. Serve in small ramekins.

SHRIMP

Lucky people of the Mississippi delta and Texas can have fresh shrimp with the heads on, but up north we must suffer those headless frozen things our merchants call shrimp. Since we must resign ourselves to frozen shrimp, let's see how best they can be used.

Tiny Shell Shrimp

These come in those sanitary-looking plastic trays, all cleaned and ready to use and only moderately expensive because many people believe that the bigger shrimp are better, which is not necessarily true. The little shrimp are best used in a hot soup or sauce without being cooked. The contact with the hot liquid is enough to cook them properly. Do not, in any case, boil them.

SMALL SHRIMP IN DANISH CUCUMBER SAUCE

Serves 4

This is a dainty first course that can be served in small pastry shells.

    1 pound tiny shrimp, fresh or frozen, peeled
    1 large cucumber, peeled, seeded and sliced into ⅛-inch-thick half-moons
    2 tablespoons butter
    Salt
    Pepper from the mill
1½ cups heavy cream
  ⅓ cup fresh chopped dill weed
  ½ teaspoon freshly grated lemon rind

1. Defrost the shrimp overnight in the refrigerator, if necessary.

2. Lightly salt the cucumber and let it stand for 15 minutes.

Drain off any liquid from it. Heat the butter and sauté the cucumber in it until all liquid has evaporated. Salt and pepper.

3. Add the cream, and reduce for 5 to 6 minutes. Add the dill and lemon rind and the shrimp. Reheat well and serve in ramekins or in pastry shells.

Tiny Shrimp in Shells

These come fresh from Maine at the earliest sign of spring in late February or early March, and can constitute such bounty that they sell for almost nothing from trucks on roadsides in our area. Some years, they are so plentiful that they sell for way below a dollar a pound. Try to prepare them as simply as possible.

MAINE SHRIMP IN THEIR SHELLS

Serves 4 to 6

This is a messy dish to eat but simple to prepare.

> 1 pound Maine shrimp in their shells
> 2 tablespoons butter or olive oil
> 1 tablespoon chopped garlic
> ¼ cup chopped parsley
> ½ teaspoon finely powdered hot pepper flakes

1. Wash the shrimp thoroughly in salt water. Drain and pat dry in paper towels. Set aside.

2. In a 10-inch skillet heat the butter or oil over medium high heat. Add garlic, cook until light golden. Add the chopped parsley and hot pepper.

3. Raise the heat and immediately add the shrimp. Stir-fry the shrimp for 3 to 4 minutes until the shrimp just stiffens. Remove from the heat and cover for 5 minutes. Eat with your fingers, a huge roll of paper towels at your side and a nice bottle of cold beer nearby.

Frozen Shrimp, Medium- to Large-Size

Defrost the shrimp in the refrigerator overnight. Whatever you plan to do with the shrimp, do not boil them, since their meat is exposed where the heads originally were. The hot water will damage it and the shrimp will become tasteless and tough. Instead, pull the veins out while the shrimp are whole and still uncooked. If a vein is not too large, it will come out all by itself when cooked; if it does not come out, do not worry. It is small and empty and will not be visible when you serve. Cook the shrimp in oil in a frying pan, shells on, so the brunt of the heat goes onto the shells, not the meat.

SHRIMP AND ZUCCHINI SALAD IN SUN-RIPENED TOMATO DRESSING

Serves 6

18 jumbo shrimp
½ cup olive oil
2 small baby zucchini, cut in ⅛-inch-thick slices
Salt
Pepper from the mill
Juice of 1 lemon
3 tablespoons chopped sun-ripened tomatoes
2 tablespoons scissored basil leaf
6 Boston lettuce leaves

1. Devein the shrimp. Heat 2 to 3 tablespoons of the olive oil in a frying pan. Cook the shrimp, 6 at a time, only until they are bright red on both sides (about 5 minutes). Remove and set aside.

2. To the same pan, add the zucchini and cook for 2 minutes. Salt and pepper. Remove to a plate.

3. Shell the shrimp, and slice them into ¼-inch-thick slanted slices. Mix with the zucchini.

4. Deglaze the pan with a drop of water, scrape well, and strain the juice into a bowl. Add the lemon juice and salt and pepper, whisk in the remaining olive oil. Toss with the shrimp and zucchini. Dot with sun-ripened tomatoes and basil leaf. Serve three shrimp on a lettuce leaf as an appetizer or light luncheon.

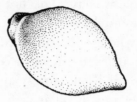

LOBSTERS AND CRAWFISH

Ours is the only country in the world where a 1¼-to-1½-pound lobster represents a single portion. In Europe, one rarely serves more than half a lobster per person. All our coasts have lobsters, and all are delicious and tender. No one tastes or looks better than another. They're all different and their meats have diverse characteristics. It is essential to differentiate between fresh lobster and frozen lobster. But all fresh lobster in my opinion, whether from Maine or Florida or California, is best steamed with a nice butter sauce as described below.

STEAMED LOBSTER WITH HERB BUTTER SAUCE

Serves 6

If you can afford it, do not hesitate to add ½ ounce of good caviar to the finished sauce. We have good caviar in America; there is no need to buy Middle Eastern or Eastern European caviar.

6 lobsters, 1¼ pounds each
½ cup lobster cooking water for the sauce
1½ tablespoons balsamic vinegar or cider vinegar
Salt
Pepper from the mill

6 tablespoons raw unsalted butter
6 tablespoons brown clarified butter
2 tablespoons chopped chervil or parsley

1. Heat 2 gallons of water in a steamer.

2. Place the lobsters in a simmer basket, cover and steam for 6 minutes. Remove from the heat and keep the pan covered another 5 minutes.

3. While the lobsters are steaming, put ½ cup of the steaming water in a pot, add the vinegar, a pinch of salt, pepper, and reduce to 3 tablespoons. On low heat, whisk in the raw butter, then the brown butter. Add the chervil or parsley and use as a dip for the steamed lobsters.

Frozen Lobster Tails

If the lobster tails are solidly frozen, do not defrost them completely, so they will retain their moisture while cooking. As soon as they melt a bit, cut out the underside membrane and start broiling on the shell side, so the tail remains flat while cooking. Broil 4 inches away from the flame for 4 minutes on the shell side and for 3 minutes on the other side, enough time to cook a lobster tail properly. Dip the lobster in butter or marinate it with any good dressing if you are going to prepare a lobster salad. The lobster tails can be replaced with any very large shrimp or with Norwegian lobster, which reaches us frozen from Europe and can be found in some larger cities.

GRILLED LOBSTER TAILS WITH SOUR CHERRY DRESSING

Serves 6

If no sour cherries are available, use 2 tablespoons of unsweetened frozen raspberries plus 2 tablespoons of red wine vinegar.

12 small lobster tails, fresh or frozen
½ cup corn oil
 3 tablespoons fresh sour cherries, pitted and chopped
 2 teaspoons red wine vinegar
 3 tablespoons heavy cream
¾ teaspoon salt
    Pepper from the mill
 2 tablespoons chopped chives
12 lettuce leaves

1. Cut out and remove the membrane from the underside of each tail. Broil the lobster tails for 4 minutes on the shell side, brush the underside with oil, and finish broiling for 3 to 4 more minutes on the underside.

2. Place sour cherries, red wine vinegar, ⅓ corn oil and heavy cream in a blender container. Add the salt, and pepper from the mill. Process until smooth, and strain to discard all traces of cherry skins. Strain into a bowl. Add the chives and correct the seasoning.

3. Shell the lobster tails. Slice each into ⅓-inch-thick slices and arrange each on a lettuce leaf. Prepare 2 tails per person. Spoon the dressing over each lobster tail while the tail is still warm. Serve at room temperature.

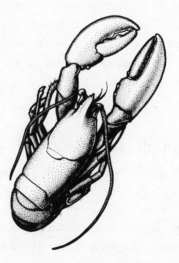

SOFT-SHELL CRABS

To be good, soft-shell crabs must be thrown in a pan while they are still alive and kicking. Coat them lightly with salted and peppered flour and cook them in either oil or butter. This is a recipe for you to enjoy.

SAUTÉED SOFT-SHELL CRABS WITH HAZELNUT BUTTER

Serves 6

     3 tablespoons flour
       Salt
       Pepper from the mill
    12 medium-size soft-shell crabs
     ½ cup raw unsalted butter
     ¼ cup chopped, toasted hazelnuts
     1 tablespoon chopped shallots
     1 tablespoon chopped fresh tarragon
     1 tablespoon chopped fresh chervil
     1 tablespoon chopped fresh parsley
     6 lemon wedges

1. Mix the flour, salt and pepper. Coat the soft-shell crabs lightly with the flour. Pat them lightly to discard any excess flour.

2. Melt 4 tablespoons of butter, add 6 crabs and fry them for 2 to 3 minutes on each side, until they are nice and crisp. Remove them to a paper towel.

3. To the same pan, add the hazelnuts. Sauté them until they turn brown and the butter has turned a dark hazelnut color. Turn off heat. Stir in shallots and fresh herbs. Serve the soft-shell crabs basted with the butter. If you wish, serve lemon wedges with each portion.

CRAWFISH, CRAWDADS, MUDBUGS

There are two types of crawfish and sweetwater lobsters. Those found in torrents and lakes in the mountains are grayish brown and live in large quantities in the lakes of old Appalachia. The kids play with them and call them crawdads or mudbugs. Being a mountain person, I love them. I think they are the best—the firmest and the sweetest ever. (In French we call them *écrevisses à pattes blanche.*) But ask a Southerner or a Texan or even a Californian, and he will tell you that his crawfish are a lot better. They certainly are bigger, and nice and firm at the beginning of the season, but as the water warms up with the spring, they become quite a bit softer. In France we call crawfish from the Bayou or the Sacramento River delta *écrevisses à pattes rouges.*

Remember that if the crawfish have been frozen the only way you can use them is in a bisque. Otherwise, the tails will be mushy and will lose all their firmness, even if you immerse them in boiling water while they are still frozen. The best way to cook crawfish is to sauté them first, then finish cooking covered.

CRAWFISH AND ARTICHOKE HEARTS ETUVÉ

Serves 6

This recipe in no way resembles the New Orleans dish, which I have toned down to suit my French-born taste buds. The artichokes and crawfish compliment each other so well.

> 2 tablespoons butter
> 2 onions, chopped
> 2 shallots, chopped
> 1 tiny carrot, chopped
> 6 dozen crawfish of your choice, washed
> 1 sprig thyme
> ½ small bay leaf, crushed

2 cups heavy cream
2 tablespoons dark rum
6 artichoke bottoms, cooked and slivered into ¼-inch-thick
slices

1. In a large pot, heat the butter, add the onions, shallots, and carrot and sauté over low heat until the onions are translucent.

2. Add the crawfish, thyme, and bay leaf and sauté briefly over medium heat (about 2 minutes). Cover and continue to cook for about 5 minutes, shaking the pot occasionally to redistribute the crawfish.

3. Using a slotted spoon, remove crawfish to a bowl and set aside.

4. To the vegetables in the pot, add the heavy cream and rum and reduce over medium high heat until you have about 1½ cups.

5. Strain sauce and return to pot. Add crawfish and artichoke bottoms and cook until just heated through.

DUCK

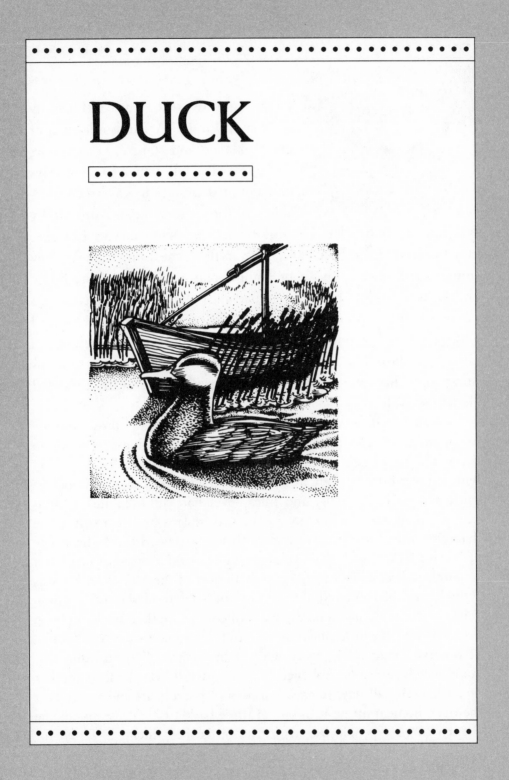

Uncle Jules was the husband of my great-aunt Orelly. A handsome man of great prestige and stature, he stood six feet five inches tall, which in those days of vitamin deprivation was a considerable size for a Frenchman. Aunt Orelly was not much smaller. He was from near Mirecourt in Lorraine and she from L'Île-Bouchard, not far from the Loire valley. They caught each other's eye for one single reason: She loved the fiddle and he was a fiddle builder. He had met Orelly while delivering a violin for the master at one of the castles around L'Île-Bouchard and after duly marrying her, had taken her back to his small *atelier* (artist's studio). The atelier smelled of wood and glue, and violins hung from the ceiling and were lined up on hooks neatly arranged along the wall.

Orelly's kingdom was an old kitchen with one of those antique bread ovens on the side of a huge chimney. She'd make bread in there. She also made giant *feouses* (the original name for a quiche) with leftover bread dough, a sliver of smoked bacon, eggs and double-thick heavy cream. Orelly and Jules never had children, and to compensate, they gave asylum to one of my cousins and to many more than one animal in the fifty years of their marriage. I think the whole of Noah's Ark must have been represented at their house at one point or another. I remember rather fondly the pet of the year 1939. He was a duck that had entered the family after a fateful day of hunting. Jules, being a sloppy shooter, had killed the mother duck, only to discover the ugly little duckling a minute or so later. It was a bundle of misery, trying to fly away with all its might. The duckling was lame, which probably explained why it had still been with its mother on such a late fall day. Jules was a man of good heart and so brought the duck home, putting it in one of those basket cage contraptions the French country people use to restrict birds they intend to fatten for the pot. When the weather grew cold, the duck was brought into the barn. One day while Jules was playing the fiddle, the duckling, which was slowly turning into a gorgeous mallard, somehow squeezed out of his wire prison and came limping into the atelier to settle at Jules's feet, listening intently. From then on the duck was baptized Julien and became part of the family. That duck was a Mozart fancier first and foremost, but he went gaga when Uncle Jules played Massenet's "Meditation" from *Thaïs,* the bravura piece of French violinists in the 1930s. Julien was a character and a sight. I can still evoke the image of him using his head to keep the beat with Jules's tune.

I went back to Paris after my two weeks in Lorraine and forgot all about Jules and Julien. My cousin told me the end of their story. Well, hate unfortunately always seems to triumph. The village *instituteur* (teacher), as in any small French village, advocated left-wing politics, and being a socialist, he was not on Uncle Jules's list of favorite people. Oh, they exchanged a glacial "Bonjour, monsieur" when they met at the center of the single village street, but that was it. Then Jules was voted in as town elder on the Catholic ticket, while the *instituteur* remained nonelected, stewing in his socialist rage. The victim was to be Julien, and it was Jules at that who was responsible. Jules had gotten into the habit of using Julien as a decoy to attract other birds on the municipal pond. So Julien took to the water and often at night would escape from the barn and go take a luxury bath all by himself. My cousin said that one early morning at 4 A.M. a single shot was heard and that Julien was never seen afterward. That was of course not proof positive. . . . The only evidence manifested was the high and mighty smell of *salmis* (duck stew) cooking, which could be picked up by whoever passed in front of the schoolmaster's door on that day. It was village hunting, nothing less, nothing more.

Uncle Jules and the *instituteur* both entered the Elysian Fields quite a while ago. Up there, they are probably reconciled, and surely sitting between them is Julien, his neck slightly crooked, listening while Mozart himself plays the fiddle.

COOKING DUCKS

You may not be that familiar with cooking duck, for I know that many Americans consider it a fancy meat that is not easy to cook at home. Do yourself a favor; start by roasting yourself a duck and enjoy it with your favorite friends. One duck yields two huge portions or four reasonable ones. If you serve six persons, use two ducks; if you serve eight to ten, use three or four. You will have some left over for a salad like the one on page 170. The best duck is available in the markets from October to March. In America we work with essentially two types of ducks: the Chinese Peking or Canton duck, the white one that has a yellow bill, and the Muscovy duck, which ranges in size from small to very large. The Muscovy can yield huge fillets, and is just becoming popular. Those huge fillets make wonderful steaks.

ROAST DUCK AMERICAN-STYLE WITH CRANBERRIES AND KUMQUATS

Serves 4 to 6

This is my favorite method of roasting a whole duck. Roast at 325° so that the fat runs slowly out of the duck and the skin becomes crisp and delicious.

> 2 ducks, 5 pounds each
> ½ pound whole kumquats and ½ pound sliced
> ½ pound cranberries, washed and sorted
> Salt
> Pepper from the mill
> 1 tablespoon light soy sauce
> ½ teaspoon honey
> 1 tablespoon water
> Sugar to taste
> 2 tablespoons Grand Marnier or other orange liqueur

1. Clean the inside of each duck carefully by rinsing it in cold water. Pat dry. Pat the inside dry. Add 3 whole kumquats and 12 cranberries to the cavity of each duck. Salt and pepper and truss or tie the birds. Preheat the oven to 325°.

2. Brush the ducks breast side up with a mixture of the soy sauce, honey and water. Put breast side up on a rack fitted over a roasting pan and bake for 40 to 45 minutes. After 35 minutes break the side just below the breast with a skewer until you feel the resistance of the meat under the skin. Put back to bake for another 2 hours.

3. While the ducks bake, put the rest of the cranberries in a pot with as much sugar as you like (⅓ of a cup may be enough), a pinch of salt and 1 cup of water. Cook over medium heat until the berries pop open and a sauce forms. Strain this to remove the skins.

4. Return the cranberry sauce to a saucepan, add the sliced kumquats and another ½ cup of water. Cook until the kumquats have softened. Add the Grand Marnier and more sugar, if you desire, plus a pinch of salt and pepper. The less sugar you use, the better the sauce.

5. While the ducks are roasting, tilt them forward to release the juices from the cavity. The ducks are done when the juices run clear from the cavity.

6. *To make the gravy:* Using a bulb baster, remove most of the fat from the roasting pan. Add enough water to barely cover the bottom of the pan, place over heat and scrape well to dissolve all the hardened juices. Strain the obtained gravy into a pan, mix it with the prepared cranberry and kumquat sauce and serve over the duck.

DUCK LEGS AND BREASTS OR FILLETS

Some supermarkets are already selling cut-up duck legs and duck breasts. If yours doesn't, encourage them to do so.

If you can't find already cut-up duck pieces in your supermarket, remember that it's as easy to cut up a duck as it is a chicken. If you decide to cut it up yourself, you'll be left with a bonus of the duck carcass, which is perfect for making a homemade duck broth. Here's a good, easy recipe.

DUCK STOCK

Yield: 1 quart

1 duck carcass, plus giblets and wings from 2 five-pound ducks
6 cups water
2 leeks
2 onions, studded with two cloves
1 carrot
6 parsley stems
1 teaspoon dried thyme
1 bay leaf
1 chicken bouillon cube

1. Using a large knife, cut the duck carcass into several large pieces. Place in a roasting pan and bake in a 375° oven for 30 minutes or until the skin and meat that remain on the bone are golden.

2. Pour off all fat from the pan. Add one cup of the water and scrape with a wooden spatula to dissolve all brown particles. Pour carcass and liquid into a large stockpot. Add the remaining ingredients, including the 5 cups of water, and simmer uncovered for about 1½ hours.

3. Allow entire mixture to cool. Strain into another pot and taste for seasonings.

4. Refrigerate and remove any fat that has settled on the surface.

GLAZED DUCK LEGS WITH APRICOT AND PISTACHIO COUSCOUS

Serves 6

A marriage of Oriental and Moroccan flavors

```
    6 duck legs
    1 tablespoon dark soy sauce
    1 teaspoon honey
    1 tablespoon Worcestershire sauce
    4 tablespoons butter
 1½ cups prepared or instant couscous (1 box)
 1¼ cups boiling water or chicken broth
    6 dried apricots, cut into slivers
   36 pistachios, peeled
  ½ cup water or broth
 1½ cup finely slivered scallions
```

1. Preheat the oven to 325°. Brush the duck legs with a mixture of the soy sauce, honey and Worcestershire sauce. Put the legs on a rack, place over a roasting pan, and roast slowly for approximately 1¾ to 2 hours, turning them once, or until the legs are a deep golden brown.

2. While the duck legs finish cooking, heat the butter in a large saucepan, add the couscous and toss together. Add the boiling water or chicken broth, remove from the heat and let stand, covered, until the couscous has absorbed all the water. Just before serving, add the slivered apricots and the pistachios so both remain crisp.

3. Remove duck legs and rack from the pan. Dissolve the

caramelized juices over medium heat with ½ cup of water or broth and reduce a bit to thicken. Strain into a small sauce bowl. Serve the legs smothered with scallions and surrounded with apricot and nut couscous.

A Modern Confit

Anything *"confit"* in France is prepared in heavy amounts of either salt or sugar for preservation. In a true confit, the meat is packed in a lot of salt, then baked in its own fat and preserved for months. This recipe does not pretend to be a true confit; it is a modern version, which I like to prepare because of the succulence of the duck legs when they are cooked in this manner. Keep all the duck fat in your freezer, as well as fat from other birds, such as geese. All those of you with family origins in Hungary, Czechoslovakia, Poland, eastern Austria and Germany know how wonderful the fat is. And let us all rejoice in the fact that duck fat is not as bad for your health as fat from beef or other large animals. You can find the reason for this in the book of my favorite colleague, Paula Wolfert, who wrote about this in *The Cooking of Southwest France.* It is a fascinating text that will be of interest to you.

Meanwhile, here is how to make a different confit that will please all your guests and leave you free to join your own cocktail hour.

CONFIT OF DUCK LEGS WITH ONIONS AND STRAWBERRY RHUBARB SAUCE

Serves 6

The confit is salted—not as heavily as in France. This is a major treat.

     6 duck legs from 5- to 6-pound ducks
     1 teaspoon ground cardamom
       Pinch of ground cloves
    ½ teaspoon ground ginger
    ¼ teaspoon allspice
    ¼ teaspoon ground cumin
     1 teaspoon dried thyme leaves
     1 large bay leaf, crumbled
     1 teaspoon fine salt
     2 quarts rendered duck fat
    24 small silver-skinned onions, peeled
    12 shallots, peeled and each broken into two balls
    24 garlic cloves, peeled
   1½ pounds rhubarb cut into 1-inch pieces
     1 cup sliced strawberries
     1 teaspoon Worcestershire sauce
     1 teaspoon honey, or more to taste

1. Place the duck legs in a shallow 2-quart glass pan. Mix the cardamom, cloves, ginger, allspice, cumin, thyme, bay leaf and fine salt and sprinkle evenly over both sides of the duck. Let marinate in the refrigerator covered with plastic wrap for 24 hours.

2. Preheat the oven to 325°.

3. Spoon the fat over the duck legs. Sprinkle the legs with the mixed onions, shallots and garlic. Place in the preheated oven. Bake until the onions and shallots are golden, about 1 hour. Remove the onions and shallots to a plate and keep them warm. Continue baking until the garlic is golden. At this point, check the doneness of the duck legs with a skewer. If the meat is done, the skewer will come out freely.

4. While the duck bakes, put the rhubarb in a saucepan and cook over very moderate heat until it falls apart and turns into a sauce, about 25 to 30 minutes. Add the strawberry slices, Worcestershire sauce and honey to your taste. Do not oversweeten—the tartness is there to cut the richness of the duck.

    5. To serve, drain the duck and onions well on paper towels. Put on a large platter with the pink rhubarb sauce.

SALMIS OF DUCK LEGS

Serves 6

In a traditional salmis, which is a stew, the bird is preroasted whole in a 400° oven, then carved and cooked in an excellent broth. Most of the time, the sauce is finished with the addition of a small amount of the duck's blood. Since this is not palatable in the United States, see how I use the liver to obtain a wonderfully rich sauce. Don't worry—you will not even taste the liver; it disappears altogether.

    6 duck legs
    3 tablespoons butter or oil
    1 large onion, sliced thickly
    1 carrot, sliced thickly
    1½ cups excellent red wine, such as Côtes du Rhône
    1½ cups duck or chicken broth
    3 parsley stems
    1 bay leaf
    ½ teaspoon dried thyme leaves
    12 small carrots, peeled
    12 small white turnips, peeled
    12 baby onions
    1 tablespoon chopped duck or chicken liver
    ½ cup chopped watercress leaves
    Watercress sprigs for garnish

    1. Brush the duck legs with 1 tablespoon of the butter or oil and brown well in a preheated 400° oven.
    2. Sauté the onion and carrot in 2 tablespoons of the butter or oil. Discard butter or oil and add the wine; reduce by one-half.

Add the broth, the parsley stems, bay leaf, thyme and the duck legs. Cover with an upside-down foil sheet. Bake in a preheated 325° oven until a skewer inserted at the thickest part of a leg comes out freely.

3. While the duck legs cook, parboil the small carrots, turnips and baby onions in boiling salted water for 10 to 12 minutes.

4. When the duck legs have cooked, remove them to a plate and keep them warm. Strain the sauce into a measuring cup and separate the lean from the fat with a baster. Discard the fat and simmer the vegetables for 5 to 6 minutes in the sauce.

5. Place the liver in a blender container, start the blender and pour the sauce into it. Process until smooth, return to the pot and let stand for 10 minutes. Reheat without boiling.

6. To serve, put the duck legs in a country-style serving dish, top them with the vegetables and sprinkle heavily with the watercress. Strain the hot sauce over the stew and, surround with watercress sprigs.

Broiled Duck Legs

You can easily prepare broiled duck legs. Be patient, though; it takes a while and things cannot be rushed. Here is a recipe to practice on.

BROILED DUCK LEGS WITH PEAR AND GINGER CHUTNEY

Serves 6

> 6 duck legs
> ⅛ teaspoon ground cloves
> ½ teaspoon allspice
>   Duck fat or oil
> 6 pears, peeled and diced
> 2 tablespoons fresh ginger, blanched and finely diced
> ½ cup Major Grey's chutney

1. Sprinkle duck legs with spices and let stand, covered, for at least 1 hour.

2. Place the duck legs on a rack fitted over a jelly-roll pan. Brush with fat or oil and broil for 10 minutes on the meat side; turn over and broil for another 7 or 8 minutes on the skin side.

3. Turn the oven down to 325° and finish cooking the duck legs by slowly roasting them until a skewer goes into a leg and comes out freely. Be patient—this will take at least another hour.

4. *To prepare the chutney:* Put the pears, ginger and chutney in a small saucepan and cook together until the pears have softened. Serve with the broiled duck legs.

Breast of Duck

Breast of duck *(magret)* is very popular in France. It can be cooked just as you would a steak.

PANFRIED BREAST OF DUCK WITH APPLES AND RADICCHIO

Serves 6

The richness of the duck meat is offset by the tartness of the radicchio and the apple.

> 6 large duck fillets, skinless
> ½ cup Calvados or applejack
> 1 pinch each of cinnamon, clove, allspice and cardamom
> 6 tablespoons butter
> 3 green apples, peeled, seeded and cut in ¼-inch thin slices
> 2 small heads radicchio
> 6 escarole leaves
> 2 tablespoons red wine vinegar
>   Salt and pepper
> ⅔ cup chicken or duck stock

1. Brush each duck fillet with a bit of the applejack or Calvados. Sprinkle a bit of the spice mixture on each side. Let stand for 30 minutes, covered, at room temperature.

2. Heat 2 tablespoons of the butter in a large skillet and in it brown the slices of apples on both sides very well. Set aside.

3. Separate the leaves of the radicchio and escarole. Bring a large pot of water to a boil, blanch the escarole leaves for 2 minutes, remove and drain. Then add the vinegar and blanch the radicchio leaves for 1 minute. Drain all on paper towels. Melt 1 tablespoon of butter and roll the leaves of both greens in hot butter, salt and pepper.

4. Heat the remaining 3 tablespoons of butter in a large skillet, add the fillets of duck and panfry them to rare, 3 to 4 minutes on each side. Season well, remove them to a plate and cover with a second plate to keep warm. The fillets will continue cooking to medium rare while you prepare the sauce.

5. Deglaze the pan with the remainder of the Calvados or applejack and the stock; reduce very well.

6. To serve, slice the fillets of duck crosswise into paper-thin slices. On a platter, alternate slices of duck with slices of apple; strain the gravy over the meat and apples. Decorate the plate with the leaves of escarole and radicchio and serve piping hot.

FILLETS OF DUCK GRILLED WITH BITTER CHOCOLATE AND HAZELNUT BUTTER

Serves 6

The addition of chocolate here acts as a binder in the sauce.

> 4 tablespoons butter or Diet Butter (see page 50)
> ½ ounce bitter, unsweetened chocolate, finely chopped
> 2 tablespoons chopped, toasted hazelnuts
>   Salt and pepper
> 6 duck fillets, skinless
> 2 tablespoons oil of your choice
> ⅔ cup excellent duck or chicken stock, reduced to ⅓ cup

1. Cream the butter, add the chocolate and hazelnuts, salt and pepper to your taste. Roll in a piece of Saran Wrap like a sausage and freeze.

2. Heat the grill. Oil the fillets of duck very well and grill them for 3 minutes on each side. Push hard on them with the lid of a pot to force the heat to their centers and then remove them to a plate. Let them stand for a few minutes before carving them.

3. Transfer the duck fillets to a platter and serve topped with paper-thin slices of chocolate butter. At the last minute, dribble the reduced stock over the fillets.

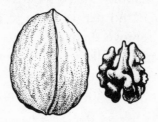

DUCK SALAD

Serves 4

This salad is excellent with roast duck leftovers, but with cold confit of duck leg it reaches wonderful heights. Also try it with smoked duck, either store-bought or your own.

   1½ cups duck meat, cut into 1-by-½-inch slivers
     3 pears, peeled and sliced
     1 head escarole, cleaned and torn into bite-size pieces
     3 Belgian endive, cut into ¼-inch slivers
   ⅓ cup chopped, toasted walnuts

FOR THE DRESSING
     1 tablespoon bourbon or armagnac
     3 tablespoons red wine vinegar
     1 teaspoon salt
   ½ teaspoon Szechuan pepper
   ⅔ cup walnut oil

1. Mix the duck meat, pears, escarole and endive.

2. Blend or process all the elements of the dressing until they are homogeneous. Toss the dressing into the salad ingredients and serve sprinkled with walnuts.

DUCK SKIN, SHALLOT AND BREADCRUMB OMELETTE

Serves 4

Duck skins are very nutritious and delicious, if after cooking them you drain them well on two paper towels.

Skin of 1 duck, cut into ¼-inch slivers
2 shallots, finely chopped
⅓ cup coarsely chopped, toasted breadcrumbs
1 tiny clove garlic, mashed
2 tablespoons chopped parsley
8 eggs
2 tablespoons butter

1. Place the duck skin slivers in water to cover and simmer until all the water has evaporated. When the water is gone the skins will crisp in their own fat. This will take at least 1 hour. Don't be impatient. Set aside the fat that has rendered in the process, to make a confit later. Place the skins on a paper towel and drain to remove all traces of fat.

2. Mix the duck skins with the shallots, breadcrumbs, garlic and parsley. In a separate bowl, beat the eggs; set aside.

3. Heat the butter in an omelette pan and quickly sauté the duck-skin mixture. Add the beaten eggs and cook into an omelette. Invert onto a plate and serve promptly.

ACCOMPANIMENTS FOR DUCK

All the grain pilafs on pages 76 to 79 are excellent, especially the barley pilaf. Here are a few side dishes that blend especially well with duck.

ASPARAGUS IN CORIANDER BUTTER

Serves 6 to 8

>   2 pounds asparagus, peeled
>   1 tablespoon lemon juice
>   ½ teaspoon lemon rind, finely grated
>   Salt and pepper
>   6 tablespoons butter
>   2 tablespoons finely chopped coriander leaves

1. Cook the asparagus in a large amount of water and then reserve ½ cup of liquid. To this ½ cup, add the lemon juice, the lemon rind, a dash of salt and pepper. Reduce the mixture to 2 table-spoons. Over low heat, whisk in the butter and add the coriander. Serve the coriander butter over the asparagus and with any dish of duck.

FIDDLEHEADS WITH DRIED MUSHROOMS

Serves 6 to 8

Fiddleheads, as you know, are ferns that we collect in New England forests when spring comes. They are available in May and June. They are excellent if you serve them in a wild mushroom butter. Use dried mushrooms rather than fresh ones, since at that time of the year there are only morels and they are so very expensive. All you need are 4 or 5 pieces that you can rehydrate in very, very little water and chop very fine. Here is the recipe.

> 4 tablespoons butter
> 4 to 5 pieces dried mushrooms, rehydrated in 2 or 3
>   tablespoons warm water
> ¾ pound fiddleheads, well cleaned and rinsed of all sand
>   and dirt from the forest
>   Salt
>   Pepper from the mill

1. Melt butter and add the mushrooms. Sauté until golden. Keep warm.

2. Cook the fiddleheads in rapidly boiling salted water for 5 minutes.

3. Add fiddleheads to the butter and mushrooms and toss well. Season with salt and pepper.

SPAETZLE

Serves 6

This is a quick way to make your own noodles. They are soft and delicious and a perfect complement to slightly crunchy stir-fried vegetables.

   2 cups flour
     Salt
     Fresh-ground black pepper
   6 eggs
   ⅓ cup chopped parsley
   2 cloves garlic, mashed to a purée
   ⅓ to ½ cup milk
   8 tablespoons butter
   6 small pickling cucumbers, sliced ¼-inch thick
   1 bunch red radishes, sliced ¼-inch thick
     Wine or cider vinegar

1. Put the flour into a large bowl; sprinkle with 1 teaspoon salt and plenty of pepper. Make a well in the center of the flour and break the eggs into it. Put ¼ cup of the parsley and the garlic on top of the eggs. Whisk the eggs, and when they are well broken up, gradually incorporate the flour to make a very thick batter. Add the milk, a small amount at a time, to make a fairly thick crepe batter.

2. Bring a large pot of water to a boil. Turn down to a simmer. Add plenty of salt to the water. Pour some of the batter onto the back of a round cake pan and with a spatula "shave" ¼-inch-wide ribbons of batter into the water. Don't cook too many at one time. The spaetzle are done when they come floating to the top. Lift them out with a slotted spoon.

3. Melt 6 tablespoons of the butter in a large warm dish. Add the drained spaetzle and toss well. Keep them warm.

4. As soon as all the batter is cooked, melt the remaining 2 tablespoons of butter in 2 separate skillets. Add the cucumbers to one skillet and the radishes to the other. Toss vegetables until warm, seasoning them with salt and pepper. Add a few drops of vinegar to the radishes to set the color.

5. Add the vegetables to the spaetzle and sprinkle with remaining parsley.

PIZZA AND PASTRY

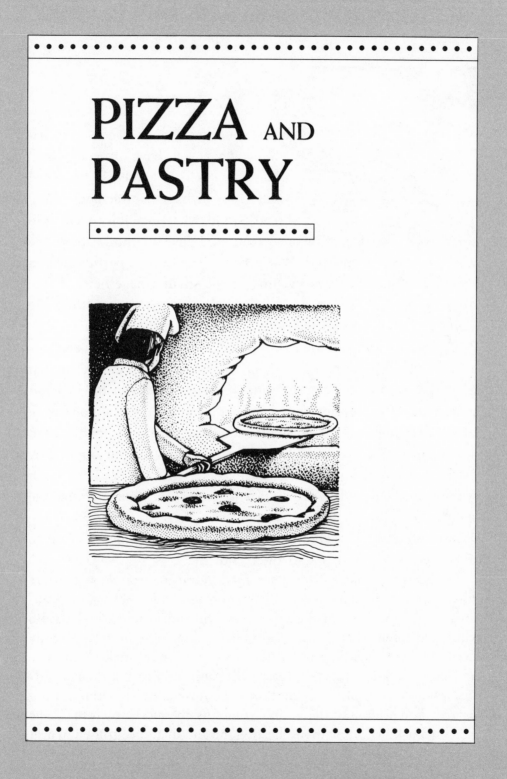

THE PIZZA PRINCIPLE

Have you ever thought about the origin of what you have in your hand when you hold a piece of bread? I often think what a miraculous thing bread is and what ingenuity went into its creation. I love to think about the way Stone Age men lived. When I was seventeen, I participated in the excavation of a cave dwelling in the small village of La Balne de Thuy in Savoie and was fascinated when in their sifting, the scientists found some dried wild grains several thousand years old. The professor who headed the dig was transported with enthusiasm about what he had found. Of course, the importance of that grain did not strike me at the time. I was to remember the incident only when I became interested in food. Since then, I've gone back to the site time and again, hoping that the excavation had started again, but the cave is covered with metal plates and surrounded by a wire fence bearing warnings to not enter. Blessed be the woman who figured out that by toasting wild grains, she could remove the shafts. Blessed be that other woman who discovered that when the grains sprouted, they became easier to digest and who went on to dry those grains and pound them into meal.

From meal mixed with water came a number of products that are still with us in many forms: the flatbreads and crackers of Scandinavia, the Mexican tortillas, the American Indian journeycakes, also known as johnnycakes. Leavened bread didn't come to us apparently until the Egyptians discovered that wild yeast could make bread rise and puff up. They discovered it only because they had at their fingertips a new variety of wheat that could be husked easily without being heated. The heating of the grain changes its chemical structure. To be able to husk wheat without heating meant that the ground wheat kernels could be used in their raw state, leaving their proteins intact, and could be worked as flour with water to create gluten. Gluten is, as most of us know, the bread maker. This protein develops when we knead a dough and trap into it all the carbon dioxide produced by the yeast, which makes the holes in the loaves.

How, then, did pizza come about? Simply. In all the cuisines of the world you will find wonderful things made with bread dough. In France we call them *galettes,* and they are made mostly with a handful of bread dough topped with whatever is available. One of the most curious is the Savoie galette covered with *la-crutz* (skimming of the butter one would melt for winter storage) mixed with a bit of honey. In Provence, the *panisses* are made of chick-pea flour and bread dough and flavored with wonderful Mediterranean flavorings such as orange-flower water and anise. In Brittany, they refine unleavened bread dough to make sweet galettes, first cousins to the Celtic and Viking butter shortbreads. I have no doubt that the idea of pastry preceded that of leavened bread. Stone Age women had wild honey and wild herbs, didn't they? The panisses of Provence may very well have been created ten thousand years ago in one of the many early settlements along the Mediterranean that have been studied. The ladies probably mixed gruel with melted animal fat, wild honey and wild herbs. There must have also been many wild oranges at that time. Flatbread topped with vegetables or fruit became a pie made with bread dough, such as the original quiche Lorraine, for which I give you the recipe on page 182. I think American cooks, with their constant need for newness, did the quiche in by adding all kinds of expensive things to it. I've always felt sorry for the poor lobster that was first shelled and rebaked into an egg custard. So you can see the whole line of thinking: First came flatbread, then pastry, then leavened bread and the idea of topping some dough with vegetables; then, as yeast and honey became more and more available, the pizza idea of dough with topping was applied to sweet dough and fruit. The more we refined our flour, the whiter the bread became and the finer and softer our pastries. It was a sophisticated seventeenth-century cook who invented, or maybe just perfected, the puff pastry. There's a simple version of it on page 194, in which you can use our wonderful American berries and citrus fruits.

SAVORY BREAD-DOUGH PIZZA

To make a good pizza, all you need to know is how to prepare the simple and uncomplicated dough that follows. Then let your imagination go and put on top of it anything you like.

SIMPLE PIZZA DOUGH (SICILIAN CRUST)

Serves 6

3 cups flour
1 envelope yeast
1½ to 2 cups warm water
2 tablespoons olive oil
1½ teaspoons salt

1. Make a well in the flour, add the yeast and the water. Mix the yeast and water well and let stand until the yeast is dissolved and starts to bubble. Add the olive oil and salt.

2. Gradually bring in the flour and work into smooth bread dough. Knead for 10 minutes, put in a covered bowl and let double in bulk.

3. Punch down and let dough rest for 10 minutes. Roll out into a 12-inch round or oval sheet. It can be topped with the filling of your choice.

GARLIC, SALT AND PARSLEY PIZZA

Serves 6

This is good as an appetizer and can be made in a large sheet—as we say in France, by the meter. Cut into squares for your guests to help themselves from the pan.

1 recipe Simple Pizza Dough (opposite)
¼ cup finely chopped garlic
1 cup coarsely chopped parsley
1 tablespoon or less kosher salt
¼ cup olive oil
 Coarsely cracked pepper

1. Prepare the pizza dough, let double in bulk and punch down. Let rest for 10 minutes.

2. Roll out into a 13-by-19-inch jelly-roll pan. Sprinkle with a mixture of the garlic and parsley, top with salt and olive oil. Let double in bulk.

3. Bake in a preheated 425° oven until the parsley is well browned, about 20 minutes.

4. Remove from the oven, then sprinkle generously with cracked pepper. Cut and serve.

PISSALADIÈRE WITH MUSSELS AND SPINACH

Serves 6

A variation on the onion pizza from Nice.

2 tablespoons olive oil
2 pounds white onions, sliced thin
2 anchovies, mashed
1 pound leaf spinach, cooked and chopped
2 tablespoons chopped, oil-cured olives
¼ cup raisins
2 tablespoons pine nuts
1 recipe Simple Pizza Dough (opposite)
2 dozen mussels, cooked
½ pound full-cream mozzarella, coarsely grated

1. Heat the olive oil in a pan, add the white onions and sauté until completely cooked and almost mushy. Add the anchovies and cooked spinach, olives, raisins and pine nuts.

2. Roll out the pizza dough to fill a 13-by-19-inch jelly-roll pan.

3. Spread the vegetable mixture over the rolled-out dough and let dough double in bulk.

4. Just before baking, dot the vegetable mixture with the mussels. Cover with mozzarella and bake in a preheated 425° oven for 10 to 12 minutes, or until the cheese starts melting and the dough is crisp.

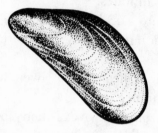

FLAMMKUCHE

Serves 6

A variation on the cream and onion pizza of the Alsace region.

2 tablespoons butter
1½ pounds yellow onions, sliced and blanched in boiling
    Water
    Salt
    Pepper from the mill
1 cup heavy cream
1 recipe Simple Pizza Dough (see page 178)
3 thin slices baked ham
2 slices thickly sliced bacon, cut into 1-inch-wide lardons

1. Heat the butter in a large skillet, add the onions, salt and pepper, and cook until very soft and almost mushy. Add the heavy cream and let reduce until the cream coats the onions.

2. Roll out the pizza dough to fit into a 13-by-19-inch jelly-roll pan.

3. Sprinkle the baked ham over the dough, add the creamed onions and spread them evenly. Dot evenly with the bacon. Bake in a preheated 425° oven until golden, about 25 minutes.

Savory Butter Bread-Dough Pizza

This dough is made in northern France for the classic *flamiche* tart. Although the other provinces represented in the recipes below use only plain bread dough, I've used a butter bread dough for added good taste and a bit of change.

BUTTER BREAD DOUGH

Serves 6

> 2 cups flour
> ⅔ cup lukewarm water
> 1½ teaspoons yeast
> 6 tablespoons melted butter
> 1 teaspoon salt

1. Make a well in the flour, add the warm water and sprinkle the yeast over it. Let stand until the yeast bubbles dough. Knead for a few minutes and immediately roll out into a 9-to 10-inch pie plate. Let rise until ¼ inch thick. Fill with your chosen filling.

FEOUSE

Serves 6

This is the recipe of my great-aunt Orelly for authentic ancient quiche Lorraine, as it was prepared in villages before it became a fashionable item. Look—no mushrooms, no shellfish, no spinach, no cheese, just plain and honest bacon and eggs.

1 recipe Butter Bread Dough (see page 181)
3 tablespoons butter
½ pound thickly sliced bacon
6 eggs
1½ cups heavy cream
Dash of nutmeg
Salt
Pepper from the mill

1. Roll out the pastry and fit it into a 9-inch pie plate, greased with 1 tablespoon of the butter. Let rise until ¼ inch thick.

2. Render the bacon until light golden but not brittle. Cut into small ¼-inch-wide pieces. Dot the dough with small pieces of butter and put the bacon on them so they remain at the bottom of the pie when you pour the custard.

3. Beat the eggs and cream together, season well with nutmeg, salt and pepper and pour over the bacon. Bake in a preheated 375° oven, 20 minutes at the bottom of the oven and 10 to 15 minutes at the top. The custard will blow up extremely high and fall afterward. Serve lukewarm.

LEEK, GOAT CHEESE AND WALNUT PIZZA

Serves 6

This recipe comes from Berry, in Menetreol-sous-Sancerre. A friend of my family taught me to prepare it with fresh goat cheese.

1 recipe Butter Bread Dough (see page 181)
4 tablespoons butter
8 medium leeks, white and light green parts only, washed
  and dried
1 cup heavy cream
  Salt
  Pepper from the mill
4 ounces goat cheese, crumbled
½ cup chopped walnuts
  Coarsely cracked pepper

1. Roll out the butter pastry and free-form it into an oval or oblong shape approximately 12 inches long and 9 inches wide. Raise the border a bit by pinching it between your fingers. Let rise while you cook the leeks.

2. Heat the butter in a large skillet, add the leeks and sauté until soft. Add the cream and cook until well reduced. Season with salt and pepper.

3. Spread the leek mixture over the bread dough and dot with the goat cheese and chopped walnuts. Bake in a preheated 425° oven until golden (about 20 minutes) and serve sprinkled with cracked pepper.

VARIATION: This is a blend of the flamiche and the gougère of Picardy in northern France. Replace the goat cheese and walnuts in the recipe with Camembert completely free of its crust and cut into ¼-inch-thick slices.

DESSERTS USING PIZZA DOUGH

PIZZA DOLCE ALL'ANTICA

Serves 6

From Latina, a city south of Rome.

> 2 tablespoons cornstarch
> 2½ cups sifted flour
> ¼ cup and 2 tablespoons warm milk
> 2 teaspoons yeast
> ½ teaspoon salt
> 3 eggs, beaten
> ½ cup olive oil
> ½ cup liquid honey
> 1 tablespoon crushed anise seeds
> ⅓ cup finely diced citron
> 1 tablespoon butter
> 1 egg yolk
> 2 tablespoons granulated sugar

1. Mix the cornstarch and the flour, make a well. Add the milk and the yeast and let stand together until the yeast bubbles.

2. Add to the well salt, beaten eggs, olive oil, honey and anise and knead together into a smooth dough. Put into a bowl and let rise until doubled in bulk. Punch down, adding the diced citron.

3. Butter well a 10-inch-round pie or pizza plate and flatten the dough evenly in it into a ½-inch-thick cake. Brush with the yolk mixed with the 2 tablespoons of milk, let rise until 1 inch thick and sprinkle with the sugar. Bake for 25 to 30 minutes in a preheated 400° oven until deep golden.

VARIATION: The city of Reims in the French Champagne district makes a similar recipe: Replace the olive oil with ½ cup of melted butter, and the anise and citron with 1½ teaspoons of orange-flower water. Top the cake with ½ cup of butter creamed with ⅓ cup of sugar just before baking. In Reims, one calls this cake a *sucrette*.

PANISSES WITH HONEY AND OLIVE OIL

Yields approximately 8 panisses

These are crunchy cookies from Orange, where the kids used to roam the streets munching on them as recently as twenty years ago. Panisses are slowly disappearing from bakeries.

> 3 cups sifted flour
> ¾ cup olive oil
> 1½ teaspoons orange-flower water
> 2 teaspoons dried orange peel
> 1 teaspoon salt
> ⅓ cup honey
> ¼ teaspoon thyme
> Water, as needed (approximately 1 cup)

1. Make a well in the flour, add the olive oil, orange-flower water, orange peel, salt, honey, and dried thyme. Add ¾ cup water and dissolve the honey in it. Gradually mix all the ingredients, adding more water as needed for consistency, until the dough holds together or forms a ball and will roll out like pie dough. Put the dough to rest in the refrigerator for thirty minutes, then roll it out into a large sheet, ¼ inch thick if you can. Cut into 3½-inch circles, pull each circle to elongate it into an oval and cut 3 slits, in the center. Bake in a preheated 375° oven until crisp, about 10 minutes. Cool and store in tins.

APRICOT TART

Serves 8

This dessert is sold in bakeries all over eastern and southeastern Switzerland.

FOR THE PIE
1 recipe Butter Bread Dough (see page 181)
2 pounds fresh apricots, pitted and halved

FOR THE TOPPING
1 egg
⅓ cup sugar or less if you desire
1 cup heavy cream
  Pinch of salt
2 tablespoons brandy of your choice (optional)

1. Prepare the butter bread dough as described on page 181. Top with apricot halves and let stand for 30 minutes at room temperature. Bake in a preheated 375° oven until the dough is deep golden and the apricots get brown tips, about 30 minutes.

2. While the apricot tart is baking, stir together the egg, sugar, heavy cream, pinch of salt, and the brandy, if desired.

3. Pour the custard mixture over the browned apricots and finish baking the tart until the custard is set, approximately 15 minutes.

ZWETSCHKEKUCHE

Serves 8

This is a sweet pizza, topped with plain white or red Italian prune plums and is served with a bowl of sweet rich cream, flavored with kirsch or plum brandy.

FOR THE PIE
2 cups sifted flour
2 tablespoons cornstarch
⅓ cup warm milk
2 teaspoons yeast
⅓ cup sugar
⅓ cup melted butter
  Pinch of salt
2 eggs, beaten
1 teaspoon cinnamon
1 teaspoon grated lemon rind
2 pounds red plums, preferably Italian prune plums

FOR THE GARNISH
¼ cup sugar
1 cup heavy cream, whipped
1½ tablespoons kirsch or plum brandy

1. Mix flour and cornstarch. Make a well in the center, and into it add the warm milk and the yeast. Let stand a few minutes or until it begins to bubble.

2. Add the sugar, melted butter, salt, beaten eggs, cinnamon and grated lemon rind and work until ingredients are incorporated, a few minutes. Add more flour if necessary to create a smooth dough, but be careful not to overwork it.

3. Place in large bowl, cover, and let double in bulk. Punch down and let rest for 10 minutes.

4. Pit the plums and cut them into quarters or halves. Roll out the dough and fit into a 10-to-12-inch pizza or pie plate. Top with the fruit and let stand for 30 minutes at room temperature.

5. Bake in a preheated 375° oven until the dough is browned and the plums have started to lose their red juices (about 40 minutes). Cool and garnish: sprinkle with 2 tablespoons of the sugar. Mix the cream with the remaining sugar and the chosen spirit and serve with the cake.

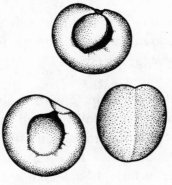

SAVORY PASTRY PIES

Look at these recipes! The bread dough has become richer with the addition of lard or butter.

RICH BACON AND RICOTTA TART

Serves 6

From Lorraine again, where bacon is ubiquitous. This recipe is from the eighteenth century.

FOR THE PASTRY
1½ cups sifted flour
½ teaspoon salt
9 tablespoons butter
1 egg, well beaten

FOR THE FILLING
2 tablespoons butter
½ pound thickly sliced bacon
¾ cup heavy cream
½ pound ricotta
2 eggs, lightly beaten
¼ teaspoon nutmeg
1 tablespoon each chopped chervil, chives, tarragon and parsley
1½ teaspoons lemon thyme

1. Mix flour and salt. Make a well n the flour. Add the butter, cut into tablespoons, and work into the flour with your fingertips. Gradually add the egg, tablespoon by tablespoon. Roll into a ball and refrigerate for 30 minutes.

2. Butter a 10-inch pie plate with 1 tablespoon of the butter. Roll out the pastry until ⅛-inch thick and fit into the plate. Line the inside of the pastry with aluminum foil, and fill with a weight (aluminum nuggets or beans), and bake for 10 minutes at 400°.

3. Render the bacon until golden but not brittle. Cut into ½-inch-wide pieces. Dot the pastry with tiny pieces of butter and sprinkle the bacon on top.

4. Discard the bacon fat and add the heavy cream to the frying pan, scraping with a wooden spoon to dissolve all the crusty bacon drippings into the cream. In a bowl, beat the ricotta, add the eggs and the flavored heavy cream as well as the nutmeg and all the herbs except the lemon thyme. Pour the cheese mixture over the bacon and sprinkle with lemon thyme. Finish baking in a preheated 375° oven until set and golden, about 20 minutes. Serve lukewarm.

MEDIEVAL MUSHROOM TART

Serves 6

An adaptation of a fourteenth-century pie.

> 1½ cups flour
> 7 tablespoons lard
> 1 teaspoon salt
> 4 to 5 tablespoons water
> 2 tablespoons butter
> 1 pound sliced mushrooms
> 1 tablespoon powdered ginger
> Salt
> Pepper from the mill
> 2 eggs
> ½ pound ricotta
> 1 tablespoon cornstarch

1. Make a well in the flour. Into it put the lard, cut in small pieces. Add salt, and work together into a meal, using 2 forks or a pastry cutter. Add the water, tablespoon by tablespoon, or until a dough forms. Let rest in the refrigerator for 30 minutes. Punch down and roll out into a 10-inch pie plate coated with 1 tablespoon of the butter. Line the inside of the pastry with foil. Add a weight (aluminum nuggets or beans) and bake for 10 minutes in a preheated 400° oven.

2. Heat the remaining butter in a skillet. Add the sliced mushrooms and sauté until brown. Add ginger, salt and pepper, and cover to extract the mushroom juices. Pour off juices and reserve.

3. Using an electric mixer beat the eggs with the mushroom juices and ricotta very well. Stir in the mushrooms. Sift in the cornstarch. Mix again. Pour into the prebaked pie shell and continue baking at 375° until the top is golden, about 20 minutes. Serve lukewarm.

SWEET DESSERT PIES

These are all modern recipes for increasingly rich pastries. In this section the pastry becomes richer and richer. What follows are variations on the basic pastry theme. Good people, make sure that these are really occasional indulgences. I only propose the recipes to you—you dispose of them. Be sure to make each of them at least once just to treat yourself. The French always say *une fois n'est pas coutume,* meaning that an occasional trip will do damage to no one.

LEMON BLUEBERRY PIE

Serves 8

The producer-director of the TV series *Madeleine Cooks* thinks this is the best lemon tart in the world.

FOR THE PASTRY
1 cup sifted flour
1 tablespoon sugar
6 tablespoons butter
1 teaspoon grated lime rind
2½ tablespoons water

FOR THE FILLING
5 tablespoons butter
½ cup sugar
1 teaspoon cornstarch
juice of 3 lemons and 2 limes
pinch of salt
½ teaspoon each grated lime rind and lemon rind
2 eggs
2 egg yolks
1 tablespoon Jack Daniel's

FOR THE TOPPING
    1 pint blueberries
    1 egg white
 ¼ cup sugar
    1 teaspoon cornstarch
 ½ teaspoon grated lime rind
    2 tablespoons lime juice
1½ tablespoons Jack Daniel's

1. Put the flour, the sugar, and the butter cut into table-spoon pieces in a food processor container. Add the lime rind and 2 tablespoons of water. Process for 55 seconds to obtain a ball of dough. Add the remainder of the water only if needed. Flatten into a ½-inch-thick, 4-inch-wide piece of dough. Refrigerate for 30 minutes.

2. To prepare the filling, cream the butter, add the sugar, cornstarch, citrus juices, salt, rinds, eggs, egg yolks, and Jack Daniel's. Mix well. If the mixture looks separated, it does not matter.

3. Roll out the pastry into an 8-inch pie plate. Prebake the shell for 10 minutes in a preheated 400° oven. Fill with the lemon cream and finish baking until golden, about 15 minutes. Cool in the pie plate.

4. Reserve 24 large blueberries. Dip 12 of them in the egg white and roll in 1 tablespoon of the sugar. Let dry on a plate. Alternate the 12 sugar-dipped berries with 12 undipped berries around the edges of the pie.

5. Mix the remaining blueberries with the remaining sugar, the cornstarch, lime rind and lime juice. Cook until a sauce forms and thickens. Serve each pie wedge with one large spoonful of the blueberry sauce.

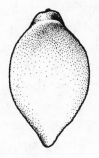

UPSIDE-DOWN PEAR PIE

Serves 8

This upside-down pie involves a bit of work but is well worth your time.

FOR THE PASTRY
¾ cup sifted flour
¼ cup finely ground walnuts
1 tablespoon sugar
4 tablespoons butter
2 to 3 tablespoons beaten egg

FOR THE FILLING
2 tablespoons butter
6 bosc or Bartlett pears, almost ripe, peeled, halved and cored
½ cup plus 2 tablespoons sugar
2 to 3 tablespoons walnut wine or red wine
12 walnut halves

FOR THE GARNISH
½ cup heavy cream whipped
2 tablespoons sugar
2 tablespoons brandy

1. Mix the flour and ground walnuts and sugar. Cut in the butter. Mix well with your fingertips and add the egg. Roll into a ball and refrigerate while the pears are baking.

2. Butter a 1½-quart baking dish with 1 tablespoon of butter. Add the pear halves. Sprinkle with sugar. Bake in a 350° oven until very brown and caramelized, about 25 to 30 minutes.

3. Butter an 8-inch pie plate with the remaining butter. Dissolve any caramelized sugar in the pear baking dish with the wine and pour into the pie plate. Add the pears and walnut halves, and pack well.

4. Roll out the pastry and put it over the pears. Roll the edges of the pastry backward to obtain a solid border when you unmold. Cut small openings in the crust with the tips of scissors to let the steam escape and bake in a preheated 375° oven for 45 minutes to 1 hour. Unmold onto a platter as soon as the pie comes out of the oven and enjoy lukewarm with whipped cream, seasoned with 2 tablespoons of sugar and the brandy.

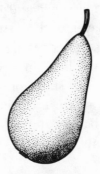

RHUBARB JULIE

Serves 8

Julie is a French lady who is alive, well, and baking pies in Paris in a commissary. She retails the pies in stores known as Tarte Julie. One of her stores is near my home in France and my son and I were excellent customers. This dessert is inspired by a tart of Julie's. *Note:* It is essential to use a Teflon or Silverstone 9-inch pie plate.

FOR THE PASTRY
½ cup and 1 tablespoon butter
½ teaspoon salt
¼ cup sugar
1 egg
1½ cups sifted flour

FOR THE FILLING
⅓ cup superfine sugar
1 pound rhubarb, peeled and cut slantwise into ⅙-inch slivers
¼ cup granulated sugar
1 teaspoon cinnamon

1. Cream the ½ cup of butter in an electric mixer. Add the salt and sugar. Beat until fluffy. Add the egg. Remove the mixer beater and, using a spatula, flatten the flour into the wet ingredients, until the dough is homogeneous. Refrigerate for 20 minutes.

2. Butter the pie plate with 1 tablespoon of butter. Sprinkle evenly with the superfine sugar and discard any excess sugar, so you have an even ⅛-inch layer. Roll out the pastry and fit into the mold over the sugar, raising the edges lightly. Arrange the rhubarb slices into concentric circles and bake in a preheated 375° oven for about 25 minutes or until the juices start coming out of the rhubarb.

3. Sprinkle a mixture of the sugar and cinnamon over the rhubarb and continue baking until the tips of the rhubarb turn deep brown. Serve lukewarm.

MODERN PUFF PASTRY

This pastry is delicious with fillings both savory and sweet. Any left-over scraps can be easily converted into delicious little cookies.

SEMI-PUFF PASTRY

Yields enough pastry for 8 Napoleons or pastry shells

This is an easy version of classic puff pastry, which I learned from cooks in Scandinavia. It combines the techniques of short pastry and classic puff pastry.

2 cups minus 1 tablespoon sifted, all-purpose, unbleached flour
1 tablespoon cornstarch
1 cup unsalted butter
¾ teaspoon salt
⅓ to ½ cup ice-cold water

1. Make a well in the flour. Add the cornstarch. Cut the butter in 1½-tablespoon chunks. Add the salt. Mash the butter into the flour with your fingers until the particles of butter are the size of whole macadamia nuts.

2. Mix in the ice water, 1 tablespoon at a time, introducing it with your fingertips. Press the small balls of dough that will form into a large one. With the heel of your hand, lightly push the ball of dough forward into large pieces and then gather it into a ball. Shape into a rectangle 6½ inches by 4½ inches. Refrigerate for 1 hour, preferably in the vegetable crisper.

3. Roll the dough 6 inches away from you and then 6 inches toward you, keeping it 6½ inches wide and never less than ⅓ inch thick. Do not bear down on the dough. Roll it out parallel to the countertop in 1 or 2 strokes. If the dough becomes wider than 6½ inches, block it on each side by placing the rolling pin parallel to the edge of the dough and tapping it gently toward the dough. The dough edge will straighten. Fold the dough in 3 folds. Turn the dough 90° so it looks like a book ready to be opened.

4. With a bit of pressure applied with the rolling pin at the top and bottom seams, pinch the layers of dough slightly to prevent the butter from escaping later. Roll out the dough again and fold it a second time, exactly as described above. You will have given it two turns. If the package of dough is less than 6 inches wide, tap it gently with the rolling pin to flatten it. To keep track of the turns, punch small depressions on the surface of the dough with your fingertips. Put the dough on a lightly floured plate. Cover it loosely with a sheet of Saran Wrap and put it to cool in the vegetable crisper of the refrigerator. The dough should rest for at least 1 hour.

5. Finish the dough by giving it two more series of two turns, exactly as described above. Rest the dough for 30 minutes between each series of turns. After turns 3 and 4, punch 4 small depressions on the surface of the dough; after turns 5 and 6, trace an X. That will remind you that the pastry is finished and may be used anytime.

6. Roll out after chilling deeply for 1 to 2 hours and cut in the shape that you desire.

PUFF PASTRY SHELLS WITH SNAILS

Serves 6 to 8

This is a modern version of a French classic.

1 dozen snails and their canning juices
½ cup butter
½ teaspoon salt
Pepper from the mill
¼ cup chopped parsley
1 shallot, grated
1 large clove garlic, mashed
¼ teaspoon nutmeg
1 recipe Semi-Puff Pastry (see page 194)
1 egg, beaten

1. Drain the snails of canning juices. Reduce the canning juices to 1 tablespoon of very thick, gelatinous liquid. Let cool. Cut each snail in half lengthwise.

2. Cream the butter. Add the cooled, reduced snail juices, salt, pepper, parsley, shallot, garlic and nutmeg. Mix well together and let the snail butter stand for 2 hours in the refrigerator.

3. Roll out the puff pastry ⅙ inch thick. Using a 2-inch-wide crinkle cutter, cut 48 circles of pastry. Dot 24 circles with a dab of snail butter, top with half a snail.

4. Brush the remaining circles of pastry with beaten egg and invert over the snails, egg side down. Cut a cross open on the top of the pastry and seal the edges well with a fork. Brush the tops with egg and bake in a preheated 425° oven for approximately 15 to 17 minutes, or until deep golden and well puffed.

5. Melt the remainder of the snail butter and spoon some into each little shell. Serve warm as an appetizer.

BERRY NAPOLEON WITH LEMON CURD

Serves 8 to 10

For Gary Danko, who sent me the Meyer lemons that allowed me to prepare this recipe.

1 recipe Semi-Puff Pastry (see page 194)

FOR THE LEMON CURD
12 egg yolks
3 cups sugar
Juice of 2 regular lemons and 6 Meyer lemons
Grated rind of 4 Meyer lemons or 4 regular lemons
1 teaspoon lime rind, finely grated
1 teaspoon orange rind, finely grated
1 teaspoon regular lemon rind, finely grated
½ cup melted butter
Confectioner's sugar
1 10-ounce package frozen raspberries

1. Cut the puff pastry in half. Roll each half into 2 sheets, each ⅛ inch thick and as wide and long as you can make it. Bake between 2 black baking sheets. Cool and cut into rectangles 1 inch by 3 inches.

2. *To prepare the lemon curd:* Beat the egg yolks with the sugar in an electric mixer until extremely thick. The mixture should form a heavy ribbon. Transfer to a large saucepan. Gradually add the lemon juice as you beat over very low heat, until the curd thickens heavily. Add all the rinds and gradually the melted butter, and cool completely.

3. *To build the napoleons:* Put the lemon curd into a pastry bag fitted with a ⅓-inch-wide, round plain nozzle. Cover 1 rectangle of pastry with an even layer of curd. Top that layer with a second rectangle of pastry. Cover that second rectangle with curd and top with a third rectangle of pastry. Powder each napoleon with confectioner's sugar.

4. Thaw the raspberries. Remove half of their syrup. Blend to a puree in the blender and strain to discard all seeds. To serve, put one napoleon on a desert plate and surround with raspberry puree. This recipe will make 8 to 10 beautiful napoleons.

VARIATION: Fresh Berry Napoleons: Instead of using just lemon curd, try the following idea. Pipe the lemon curd between the layers, as in the recipe, but add strawberries on the first layer, blueberries on the second, and raspberries on the third. Do not serve with the raspberry sauce; the berries will make their own sauce as you eat the napoleons.

INDEX

Air-Dried or Smoked Meat and Melon Salad, 99-100
Almonds
  and Ham, Jambonettes Stuffed with, 30-32
  slivered, 29
Apples with Radicchio, Panfried Breast of Duck and, 168-169
Apricot(s)
  and Ginger, Chicken Cutlets with, 7-8
  and Pistachio Couscous, Glazed Duck Legs with, 163-164
  Tart, 185-186
Artichoke Heart, Crawfish and, Etuvé, 154-155
Asparagus
  in Coriander Butter, 172
  Salad, Spinach and, 87-88
  Salmon and Dill Salad, 108
Autumn Chicken and Fruit Salad, 100-101
Avocado
  Citrus and Greens Salad, 94-95
  Lobster and Papaya Salad, 104-105

Bacon
  Bits Salad, Pear and, 91-92
  Chicken Cutlets with Mushrooms and, 8-9
  and Ricotta Tart, Rich, 188-189
  and Smoked Salmon Butter, Grilled Salmon with, 132-133
Bag cooking, whole chicken, 20-23
Bag steaming, 9
Basil
  Butter, Sautéed Green Beans in, 28, 37
  -and-Lime Marinated Chicken Thighs, 28-29
  and Zucchini, Whole Chicken in a Bag with, 22-23

Basque Style Mussel Soup, 142
Bass, Baked Striped, with Sorrel Hollandaise, 131-132
Bauer, Michael, 51
Béarnaise Sauce, Red Wine, 48-49
  Pan Roasted Tenderloin with, 47-48
Berry Napoleon with Lemon Curd, 197-198
Bierchermuesli, 65
Bistro-Style Salt-Pan Broiled Steak, 49-50
Bitter-Green Salad, Italian, 88-89
Blade Steak, 44, 45
Blueberry Lemon Pie, 190-191
Bocuse, Paul, 42
Bourbon Bulgur Pilaf, 78
Broccoli Salad, Smoked Trout and, 110
Broiling, 53
  salt-pan, 49-50
Broth (stock)
  Chicken, Homemade, 5-6
  Duck, 162-163
  Fish (fumet), 123
  Red Parsleyed Potatoes Cooked in, 57
Bulgur
  Cutlets, 78-79
  Pilaf, Bourbon, 78
Butter
  Basil, Sautéed Green Beans in, 28, 37
  Coriander, Asparagus in, 172
  Diet, 50
  Gorgonzola, Grilled Swordfish with, 133
  Hazelnut
    Fillet of Duck Grilled with Bitter Chocolate and, 169-170
    Sautéed Soft-Shell Crabs with, 153
  Noisette (browned), 118
    Breaded Chicken Cutlets with, 16-17
  Pineapple, Poached Skate Wings with, 125-126

Smoked Salmon and Bacon, Grilled Salmon
    with, 132-133
Walnut and Roquefort, 53
Butternut Squash, Grilled, and Rutabaga, 35-36

Camembert, 63
Carrots and Zucchini, Stir-Fried, with Dill, 28,
    38
Celery, Raisins and Walnuts, 39
Celery Root (celeriac), Julienne of, 39
Champagne Sauce, Stir-Fried Deep-Sea
    Scallops with, 139-140. See also King
    Fish and Emperor Wine
Chateaubriand, 44
Cheese
    Camembert, 63
    Goat, Leek and Walnut Pizza, 182-183
    Walnut and Roquefort Butter, 53
Cherry Dressing, Sour, Grilled Lobster Tails
    with, 151-152
Chicken, 1-40. See also Vegetable
    accompaniments
    American, drawbacks, 2-3
    bag cooking (whole), 20-23
        for a crowd, 23
        Mushroom, 21-22
        with Zucchini and Basil, 22-23
    breasts, boning, 4-5
    broiled (whole), 17
        Estruscan Style, 18-19
        Tunisian Style, 19-20
    Broth, Homemade, 5-6
    Cutlets, 4-17
        with Apricots and Ginger, 7-8
        Bag Steaming, 9-10
        Breaded, with Noisette Butter, 16-17
        with Coriander and Lime, 9-10
        Grilled, with Cranberry Compote, 11-12
        Grilled, with Red Plum Mustard, 13-14
        panfrying, 14
        pan steaming, 7
        Pecan-coated, with Ham, 14-16
        stove-top grilling, 11
    "frogging," 18, 19
    legs, 24-34
        boning, 32
        Broiled, with Mustard Crumb Coating,
            27-28
        Roasted, with Cucumbers, 26-27
        Roasted, with Mushrooms and Sherry,
            24-25
        Sauté, with Macadamia Nuts and
            Pineapple, 29-30

tips on roasting, 24
    with Zucchini, 25-26
Salads
    Autumn, and Fruit, 100-101
    Warm Liver, 101-102
sautéeing, 29
skin, removing, 33
Stew or Fricassee, 32-33
    Dark Meat, with Dill and Lemon, 33-34
Suprêmes, 2
Thighs, Lime-and-Basil Marinated, 28-29
Chicken Steak, 44
Chocolate, Bitter, and Hazelnut Butter, Fillet
    of Duck Grilled with, 169-170
Cholesterol, fish lowers, 112
Christmas Mixed-Grain and Nut Salad, 97
Chutney, Ginger and Pear, Broiled Duck Legs
    with, 167-168
Citrus, Avocado and Greens Salad, 94-95
Clams
    on the half-shell, 143
        Grilled Littlenecks, 143
    substitute for mussels, 140
Cod, Salt-Water-Poached, 124-125
Cognac Sauce, Steamed Mussels with Saffron
    and, 141
Compote, Cranberry, 12
    Grilled Chicken Cutlets with, 11-12
Confit, 164
    of Duck Legs with Onions and Strawberry
        Rhubarb Sauce, 165
Coriander
    Butter, Asparagus in, 172
    and Lime, Chicken Cutlets with, 9-10
Corn Grits with Okra and Squashed
    Tomatoes, 69-70
Couscous, Apricot and Pistachio, Glazed Duck
    Legs with, 163-164
Cousteau, Jacques, 112
Crabs, soft-shell, 153
    Sautéed, with Hazelnut Butter, 153
Cranberry(ies)
    Compote, 12
        Grilled Chicken Cutlets with, 11-12
    and Kumquats, Roast Duck American Style
        with, 160-161
Crawfish (crawdads, mudbugs), 137, 150, 154
    and Artichoke Hearts Etuvé, 154-155
Cream
    Endive, Grilled Oysters with, 145
    Parmesan, Polenta with Spinach and, 70-71
    Potato Gratin, 51, 59
Cucumber(s)

and Fruit Salad, Danish, 93-94
    Roasted Chicken Legs with, 26-27
    Sauce, Danish, Small Shrimp in, 147-148
Cutlets, Bulgur, 78-79. *See also* Chicken

Danish Cucumber Sauce, Small Shrimp in,
    147-148
Danish Fruit and Cucumber Salad, 93-94
Danko, Gary, 197-198
Desserts. *See* Pastry; Pizza
Diet Butter, 50
Dill
    and Lemon, Dark Meat Chicken Fricassee
        with, 33-34
    Salmon and Asparagus Salad, 108
    Stir-Fried Carrots and Zucchini with, 28, 38
Dough
    Butter Bread (Pizza), 181
    Simple Pizza, 178
Duck, 157-173. *See also* Vegetable
        accompaniments
    about, 160
    breasts (fillets), 162, 168-170
        Grilled, with Bitter Chocolate and
            Hazelnut Butter, 169-170
        Panfried, with Apples and Radicchio,
            168-169
    confit, 164
    legs, 162-168
        broiled, 167
        Broiled, with Pear and Ginger Chutney,
            167-168
        Confit, with Onions and Strawberry
            Rhubarb Sauce, 164-166
        Glazed, with Apricot and Pistachio
            Couscous, 163-164
        Salmis of, 166
    Roast, American style, with Cranberries and
        Kumquats, 160-161
    Salad, 170-171
        Warm Liver, 101-102
    salmis, 159
    Skin, Shallot and Breadcrumb Omelette,
        171-172
    Stock, 162-163

Emperor Wine, King Fish and, 122-123
Enchanted Broccoli Forest, The, 63
Endive Cream, Grilled Oysters with, 145
Escabeche
    Ocean Perch or Snapper, Chilled, 120-121
    Red Snapper Fillet, 119-120
Etruscan Style Broiled Chicken, 18-19

Etuvé, Crawfish and Artichoke Hearts,
    154-155
Eye of round, 45

Feouse (quiche), 158, 182
Fiddleheads with Dried Mushrooms, 173
Finnan Haddie
    Milk-Poached, 127
    and Potato Salad, 109
Fish, 111-133. *See also* Shellfish
    Court Bouillon, 124, 125
    foil steamed, 116-117
        Halibut, Southern California, 118
        Salmon Medallions Mamie Soleil, 117-118
    Fumet (Broth), 123
    Grilled, 132
        Salmon with Smoked Salmon and Bacon
            Butter, 132-133
        Swordfish with Gorgonzola Butter, 133
    lowers cholesterol, 112
    Oriental techniques, 113
    Oven-baked, 130
        Fillet of Sole with Provençal Flavors,
            130-131
        Striped Bass with Sorrel Hollandaise,
            131-132
    Panfried, 127
        Fillet of Trout with Bacon, 129-130
        Italian Sardines, 128
        Merluzzo Italiano, 128-129
    Pan Steamed, 119
        Chilled Ocean Perch or Snapper Fillet
            Escabeche, 120
        King Fish and Emperor Wine, 122-123
        Mountain Trout Fillets, 121
        Red Snapper Fillet Escabeche, 119-120
    Poached, 124
        Cod or Pollack Steaks, Salt-Water,
            124-125
        Finnan Haddie, Milk-, 127
        Skate Wings with Pineapple Butter, 125
    salads, 108-110
        Finnan Haddie and Potato, 109
        Salmon, Asparagus and Dill, 108
        Smoked Trout and Broccoli, 110
    salmon medallions, forming, 114
    vapor steamed salmon medallions, 114
        in Lettuce Leaves, 115-116
        in Plastic Wrap, 114-115
Flammkuche, 180-181
Flower Salad, Greens, Fruit and, 92-93
Foil-steamed fish, 116-118
    Halibut, Southern California, 118

Salmon Medallions Mamie Soleil, 117-118
Fricassee, Chicken, 32-33
  Dark Meat, with Dill and Lemon, 33-34
Fruit, choosing, 91. *See also* Salad(s)
Fumet, Fish, 123

Garlic
  Salt and Parsley Pizza, 178-179
  Sauce, Two-, 82
    Wild Rice Timbales with, 81
Geneva, 43
Ginger
  Chicken Cutlets with Apricot and, 7-8
  and Pear Chutney, Broiled Duck Legs with, 167-168
Glazed Duck Legs with Apricot and Pistachio Couscous, 163-164
Gnocchi
  cooking grains for, 67
  Semolina, with Ratatouille, 71-72
Goat Cheese, Leek and Walnut Pizza, 182-183
Gorgonzola Butter, Grilled Swordfish with, 133
Grains, 61-82
  Bulgur Cutlets, 78-79
  Corn Grits with Okra and Squashed Tomatoes, 69-70
  gnocchi
    cooking technique, 67
    Semolina, with Ratatouille, 71-72
  oatmeal
    and Fresh Fruit *(Bierchermuesli)*, 65
    porridge, 62
  pilaf(s)
    Barley and Mushroom, 77-78
    Bourbon Bulgur, 78
    cooking grains for, 76
    Salad, Warm Wehani Rice, 79-80
  polenta
    Concia, 68-69
    cooking technique, 67
    with Spinach and Parmesan Cream, 70-71
  risotto
    cooking technique, 73
    with Radicchio, 75-76
    Vegetarian, 74-75
  salad(s), 96-97
    Christmas Mixed-Grain and Nut, 97
    cooking technique, 66
    Mixed, and Vegetables, 66-67
    Provençal Rice, 96
  /water ratios, cooking, 76
  wild rice
    Timbales with Two-Garlic Sauce, 81

water fluffing, 80
Gratin, Potato, 57-59
  Cream, 51, 59
  Stock, 51, 58
Green Beans in Basil Butter, 28
Green Peppercorn Salad, Shrimp and, 106
Greens, salad. *See* Salad(s)
Grilling. *See* Chicken; Fish; Steak
Grits, Corn, with Okra and Squashed Tomatoes, 69-70

Halibut, Southern California Foil-Steamed, 118
Ham
  and Fruit Salad, 98-99
  Jambonettes Stuffed with Almonds and, 30-32
  Pecan-coated Chicken Cutlets with, 14-16
Hazelnut(s). *See also* Noisette butter
  Butter
    Fillet of Duck Grilled with Bitter Chocolate and, 169-170
    Sautéed Soft-Shell Crabs with, 153
    Stir-fried Zucchini and, 37
Honey and Olive Oil, Panisses with, 185
Horseradish, Wasabi, 113

Italian Bitter-Green Salad, 88-89
Italian Sardines, Panfried, 128

Jambonettes Stuffed with Almonds and Ham, 30-32

King Fish and Emperor Wine, 122-123
Kiwi, Turkey, and Orange Salad with Szechuan Pepper Dressing, 103-104
Kumquats and Cranberries, Roast Duck American Style with, 160-161

Leek, Goat Cheese and Walnut Pizza, 182-183
Lemon(s)
  Blueberry Pie, 190-191
  Curd, Berry Napoleon with, 197-198
  Dark Meat Chicken Fricassee with Dill and, 33-34
  Meyer, 92-93, 197-198
Lettuce, 84
  Leaves, Salmon Medallions Vapor Steamed in, 114-115
Lime
  and-Basil-Marinated Chicken Thighs, 28-29
  Chicken Cutlets with Coriander and, 9-10
Littlenecks, Grilled, on the Half-Shell, 143
Liver Salad, Warm Chicken or Duck, 101-102
Lobster, 136, 137, 150-152
  Papaya and Avocado Salad, 104-105

Steamed, with Herb Butter Sauce, 150-151
tails, frozen, 151
  Grilled, with Sour Cherry Dressing,
    151-152

Macadamia Nuts and Pineapple, Chicken-Leg
  Sauté with, 29-30
Maine Shrimp in Their Shells, 148
Marinade, Venisoned Steak, 53-54
Marinated Chicken Thighs, Lime-and-Basil,
  28-29
Meat salads. *See* Salad(s)
Medieval Mushroom Tart, 189
Merluzzo Italiano, 128-129
Meyer lemons, 92-93, 197-198
Michael's Grilled Steak, 51-52
Mignonnette, 144
Milk-Poached Finnan Haddie, 127
Mountain Trout Fillets, 121
Mushroom(s)
  and Bacon, Chicken Cutlets with, 8-9
  Chicken in a Bag, 21-22
  Dried, Fiddleheads with, 173
  and Sherry, Roasted Chicken Legs with,
    24-25
  Tart, Medieval, 189
Mussels, 137
  clams as substitute, 140
  Pissaladière with, and Spinach, 179-180
  Soup, Basque Style, 142
  Steamed
    Marinière, 140-141
    with Saffron and Cognac Sauce, 141
Mustard
  Crumb Coating, Broiled Chicken Legs with,
    27-28
  Red Plum, 13-14
    Grilled Chicken Cutlets with, 13
Mustard Greens, Wilted, and Cherry
  Tomatoes, 36

Napoleon, Berry, with Lemon Curd, 197-198
Noisette Butter, 118. *See also* Hazelnut(s)
  Breaded Chicken Cutlets with, 16-17
Nut Salad, Christmas Mixed-Grain and, 97

Oatmeal and Fresh Fruit *(Bierchermuesli),* 65
Oils, salad, 85
Okra and Squashed Tomatoes, Corn Grits
  with, 69-70
Olive oil, 85
  Panisses with Honey and, 185
Olympia Oysters with Vinegared Radish, 146
Omelette, Duck Skin, Shallot and
  Breadcrumb, 171-172

Orange, Turkey and Kiwi Salad with Tea and
  Szechuan Pepper Dressing, 103-104
Oven-baked fish, 130
  Baked Striped Bass with Sorrel Hollandaise,
    131-132
  Fillet of Sole with Provençal Flavors,
    130-131
Oysters
  Grilled, with Endive Cream, 145
  on the Half-Shell, 143, 144
  Maine Belon, 145
  Olympia, with Vinegared Radish, 146

Pan broiling, salt-, 49-50
Pancetta, 129
Panfrying. *See* Fish; Steak
Panisses, 177
  with Honey and Olive Oil, 185
Pan steaming. *See* Fish
Papaya, Lobster and Avocado Salad, 104-105
Parmesan Cream, Polenta with Spinach and,
  70-71
Parsleyed Red Potatoes Cooked in Broth, 57
Parsley, Garlic and Salt Pizza, 178-179
Pastry, 175-177, 185-197. *See also* Pizza
  galettes, 177
  history, 176-177
  panisses, 177
    with Honey and Olive Oil, 185
  Puff, 177, 194-197
    Berry Napoleon with Lemon Curd,
      197-198
    Semi-, 194-195
    Shells with Snails, 196
  savory pies, 187-189
    Medieval Mushroom Tart, 189
    Rich Bacon and Ricotta Tart, 188-189
  sweet dessert pies, 190-193
    Lemon Blueberry, 190-191
    Rhubarb Julie, 193
    Upside-Down Pear, 192
Pear
  and Bacon Bits Salad, 91-92
  and Ginger Chutney, Broiled Duck Legs
    with, 167-168
  Pie, Upside-Down, 192
Pecan-Coated Chicken Cutlets with Ham,
  14-16
Peppercorns, Green, and Shrimp, Salad, 106
Perch, Chilled Ocean, Escabeche, 120-121
Pies. *See* Pastry
Pilaf
  Barley and Mushroom, 77-78
  Bourbon Bulgur, 78

cooking technique, 76
Salad, Warm Wehani Rice, 79-80
Pineapple
    Butter, Poached Skate Wings with, 125-126
    Chicken-Leg Sauté with Macadamia Nuts
        and, 29
Pissaladière with Mussels and Spinach, 179-180
Pistachio(s)
    and Apricot Couscous, Glazed Duck Legs
        with, 163-164
    Stir-Fried Bay Scallops with, 138-139
Pizza, 175-185. *See also* Pastry
    dessert, 184-187
        Apricot Tart, 185-186
        Dolce All'Antica, 184
        Panisses with Honey and Olive Oil, 185
        Zwetschkekuche, 186-187
    Flammkuche, 180-181
    history, 176-177
    savory bread dough, 178-180
        Garlic, Salt and Parsley, 178-179
        Pissaladière with Mussels and Spinach,
            179-180
        Simple Dough (Sicilian Crust), 178
    savory butter bread-dough, 181-182
        Butter Bread Dough, 181
        Feouse (quiche), 158, 182
        Leek, Goat Cheese and Walnut, 182
Plastic Wrap, Salmon Medallions Vapor
    Steamed in, 114-115
Plums. *See* Red Plum Mustard
Poaching. *See* Fish
Polenta
    Concia, 68-69
    cooking grains for, 67
    with Spinach and Parmesan Cream, 70-71
Pollack, Salt-Water-Poached, 124-125
Porterhouse Steak, 44, 45
Potato accompaniments for steak
    Gratins, 57-59
        Cream, 51, 59
        Stock, 51, 58
    Red Parsleyed Potatoes Cooked in Broth, 57
    Rissolé, 55-56
    Swiss Baked, 55
Potato Salad, Finnan Haddie and, 109
Provençal dishes
    Fillet of Sole, 130-131
    Rice Salad, 96
Puff Pastry, 194-197
    Berry Napoleons with Lemon Curd,
        197-198
    Semi-, 194-195

Shells with Snails, 196
Quiche *(feouse),* 158, 182
Radicchio, Panfried Breast of Duck and
        Apples with, 168-169
Radish, Vinegared, Olympia Oysters with, 146
Raisins, Celery and Walnuts, 39
Ratatouille, Semolina Gnocchi with, 71-72
Red Parsleyed Potatoes Cooked in Broth, 57
Red Plum Mustard, 13-14
    Grilled Chicken Cutlets with, 13
Red Snapper Fillet Escabeche, 119-120
    Chilled, 120-121
Rhubarb
    Julie, 193
    Strawberry Sauce, Confit of Duck Legs with
        Onions and, 165-166
Rib Steak, 44
Rice
    salad
        Provençal, 96
        Warm Wehani Pilaf, 79-80
    Wild
        Timbales with Two-Garlic Sauce, 81
        water fluffing, 80
Ricotta and Bacon Tart, Rich, 188-189
Risotto
    cooking technique, 73
    with Radicchio, 75-76
    Vegetarian, 74-75
Rissolé Potatoes, 55-56
Roquefort Butter, Walnut and, 53
Rutabaga, Grilled Butternut Squash and, 35-36

Saffron and Cognac Sauce, Steamed Mussels
        with, 141
Salad(s), 83-110
    fish, 108-110
        Finnan Haddie and Potato, 109
        Salmon, Asparagus, and Dill, 108
        Smoked Trout and Broccoli, 110
    grain, 96-97
        Christmas Mixed-Grain and Nut, 97
        cooking technique, 66
        Mixed, and Vegetables, 66-67
        Provençal Rice, 96
    greens, 84
    meat, 99-104
        Air-Dried or Smoked Meat and Melon,
            99-100
        Autumn Chicken and Fruit, 100-101
        Duck, 170-171
        Ham and Fruit, 98-99
        Smoked Turkey, 102-103

Turkey, Orange, and Kiwi, with Tea and
Szechuan Pepper Dressing, 103-104
Warm Chicken or Duck Liver, 101-102
oils and vinegars, 85
shellfish, 104-110
Lobster, Papaya and Avocado, 104-105
Scallop, Warm, 107
Shrimp and Green Peppercorn, 106
Shrimp and Zucchini, in Sun-Ripened
Tomato Dressing, 149-150
simple, 87-90
Bitter-Green, Italian, 88-89
Classic Green, 87
Spinach and Asparagus, 87-88
Tomato, with Walnut Dressing, 89-90
tips, 86
Vegetable and Fruit, 91-95
Avocado, Citrus, and Greens, 94-95
Danish Fruit and Cucumber, 93-94
Greens, Fruit, and Flower, 92-93
and Mixed Grain, 66-67
Pear and Bacon Bits, 91-92
Warm Wehani Rice Pilaf, 79-80
Salmis, 159
Duck Legs, 166-167
Salmon
Asparagus and Dill Salad, 109
Grilled, with Smoked Salmon and Bacon
Butter, 132-133
Vapor Steamed
in Lettuce Leaves, 115-116
in Plastic Wrap, 114-115
Salt
Garlic and Parsley Pizza, 178-179
-pan broiling, 49-50
-Water-Poached Cod or Pollack Steaks,
124-125
Sardines, Panfried Italian, 128
Sauce
Béarnaise, Red Wine, 48-49
Pan Roasted Tenderloin with, 47-48
Champagne, Stir-Fried Deep Sea Scallops
with, 139-140
Danish Cucumber, Small Shrimp in, 147
Endive Cream, Grilled Oysters with, 145
Hollandaise, Baked Striped Bass with
Sorrel, 131-132
Red Wine, Classic Panfried Steak with,
46-47
Saffron and Cognac, Steamed Mussels with,
141
Strawberry Rhubarb, Confit of Duck Legs
with Onions and, 165-166

Two-Garlic, 82
Wild Rice Timbales with, 81
Wine, Emperor, King Fish and, 122-123
Scallop(s), 138
Salad, Warm, 107
Stir-Fried, 138
Bay, with Pistachios, 138-139
Deep Sea, with Champagne Sauce,
139-140
Semolina Gnocchi with Ratatouille, 71-72
Seviche. See Escabeche
Shallot, Duck Skin and Breadcrumb Omelette,
171-172
Shellfish, 135-155. See also Fish
Clams, 143
Grilled Littlenecks, on the Half-Shell, 143
crawfish (crawdads, mudbugs), 137, 150, 154
and Artichoke Hearts Etuvé, 154-155
lobster, 136, 137
with Herb Butter Sauce, 150-151
Papaya and Avocado Salad, 104-105
tails, frozen, 151
Tails, Grilled, with Sour Cherry
Dressing, 151-152
mussel(s), 137
clams as substitute, 140
Soup, Basque Style, 142
mussels, steamed (or clams), 140
Marinière, 140-141
with Saffron and Cognac Sauce, 141
oysters, 143
Grilled, with Endive Cream, 145
on the Half Shell, 144
Olympia, with Vinegared Radish, 146
regional, 137
Scallop Salad, Warm, 107
scallops, stir-fried, 138-140
Bay, with Pistachios, 138-139
Deep Sea, with Champagne Sauce,139-140
shrimp, 147-150
frozen, medium- to large-size, 149
and Green Peppercorn Salad, 106
Maine, in Their Shells, 148
Small, in Danish Cucumber Sauce,
147-148
tiny, in shells, 148
tiny shell, 147
and Zucchini Salad in Sun-Ripened
Tomato Dressing, 149-150
soft-shell crabs, 153
Sautéed, with Hazelnut Butter, 153
Sherry and Mushrooms, Roasted Chicken Legs
with, 24-25

Shrimp, 147-150
    frozen, medium- to large-size, 149
    and Green Peppercorn Salad, 106
    Maine, in Their Shells, 148
    Small, in Danish Cucumber Sauce, 147-148
    tiny, in shells, 148
    tiny shell, 147
    and Zucchini Salad in Sun-Ripened Tomato
        Dressing, 149-150
Sicilian Crust (Simple Pizza Dough), 178
Sirloin Steak, 44
Skate Wings, Poached, with Pineapple Butter,
    125-126
Skirt Steak, 45
Smoked Meat and Melon Salad, 99-100
Smoked Salmon and Bacon Butter, Grilled
    Salmon with, 132-133
Smoked Trout and Broccoli Salad, 110
Smoked Turkey Salad, 102-103
Snails, Puff Pastry Shells with, 196
Sole, Fillet of, with Provençal Flavors, 130-131
Soleil, Mamie, Salmon Medallions, 117-118
Sorrel Hollandaise, Baked Striped Bass with,
    131-132
Soup, Mussel, Basque Style, 142
Sour Cherry Dressing, Grilled Lobster Tails
    with, 151-152
Spaetzle, 173-174
Spinach
    and Asparagus Salad, 87-88
    Pissaladière with Mussels and, 179-180
    Polenta with, and Parmesan Cream, 70-71
Squash, Grilled Butternut, and Rutabaga,
    35-36
Steak, 41-59. See also Potato accompaniments
        for steak
    blade (chicken), 42, 44, 45
    broiling, 53
    Chateaubriand, 44
    choosing, 44-45
    eye of round, 45
    grilled, stove-top, 51-53
        Michael's, 51-52
        with Walnut and Roquefort Butter, 52-53
    panfried, 45
        with Red Wine Sauce, 46-47
    pan roasted, 47
        Tenderloin with Red Wine Béarnaise
            Sauce, 47-49
    porterhouse, 44, 45
    prime cf. choice, 44
    rib, 44, 45
    Salt-Pan Broiled, Bistro-Style, 49-50

    Diet Butter for, 50
    sirloin, 44
    skirt, 42, 44, 45
    strip, 44
    tenderloin, 44, 45
    Venisoned, 53-54
Stew(s)
    chicken, 32-33
    duck (confit), 164-166
Stir-frying scallops, 138
Stock. See Broth (stock)
Stock Potato Gratin, 51, 58
Stove-top grilling. See Steak
Strawberry Rhubarb Sauce, Confit of Duck
        Legs with Onions and, 165-166
Striped Bass, Baked, with Sorrel Hollandaise,
    131-132
Strip Steak, 44
Swiss Baked Potatoes, 55, 56
Szechuan Pepper Dressing, Turkey, Orange
        and Kiwi Salad with, 103-104

Tart
    Medieval Mushroom, 189
    Rich Bacon and Ricotta, 188-189
Tea and Szechuan Pepper Dressing, Turkey,
        Kiwi and Orange with, 103-104
Tenderloin, 44, 45
    Pan Roasted, witih Red Wine Béarnaise
        Sauce, 47-49
Tomato(es)
    Cherry, Wilted Mustard Greens and, 36
    choosing, 89
    Dressing, Sun-Ripened, Shrimp and
        Zucchini in, 149-150
    Salad with Walnut Dressing, 89-90
    Squashed, Corn Grits with Okra and, 69-70
Trout
    Fillet
        with Bacon, 129-130
        Mountain, 121
    Smoked, and Broccoli Salad, 110
Tunisian Style Broiled Chicken, 19-20
Turkey Salad
    Orange and Kiwi, with Tea and Szechuan
        Pepper Dressing, 103-104
    Smoked, 102-103

Upside-Down Pear Pie, 192

Vegetable accompaniments. See also Potato
        accompaniments for steak; Salad(s)
    for chicken
        Celery, Raisins, and Walnuts, 39

Grilled Butternut Squash and Rutabaga,
    35-36
Julienne of Celery Root, 39
Sautéed Green Beans in Basil Butter, 28,
    37
Stir-fried Carrots and Zucchini with Dill,
    28, 38
Stir-fried Zucchini and Hazelnuts, 37
Wilted Mustard Greens and Cherry
    Tomatoes, 36
for duck
    Asparagus in Coriander Butter, 172
    Fiddleheads with Dried Mushrooms, 173
    Spaetzle, 173-174
Vegetarianism, 63
Vegetarian Risotto, 74-75
Venisoned Steak, 53-54
Vinegared Radish, Olympia Oysters with, 146
Vinegars, 85

Walnut(s)
    Dressing, Tomato Salad with, 89-90

Raisins and Celery, 39
and Roquefort Butter, 53
Wasabi, 113
Whiting, Merluzzo Italiano, 128-129
Wine
    Champagne Sauce, Stir-Fried Deep-Sea
        Scallops with, 139-140
    Emperor, King Fish and, 122-123
    Red
        Béarnaise Sauce, 47-49
        Classic Panfried Steak with, 46-47

Zucchini
    and Basil, Whole Chicken in a Bag with,
        22-23
    Roasted Chicken Legs with, 25-26
    and Shrimp Salad in Sun-Ripened Tomato
        Dressing, 149-150
    Stir-Fried
        and Carrots with Dill, 28-38
        and Hazelnuts, 37
Zwetschkekuche, 186-187

A NOTE ABOUT THE AUTHOR

●●●●●●●●●●●●●●●●●●●●●●●●●●●

Born in Paris, MADELEINE KAMMAN as a young woman worked in her aunt's two-star restaurant in the Loire Valley. Chez La Mere Madeleine, the restaurant she ran in Boston from 1975 to 1979, was considered by many to be one of the finest in the country. Paul Bocuse called it "the best restaurant in the United States."

She has recently moved to Glen, New Hampshire, where she continues to teach, and where she has launched a new restaurant, L'Auberge Madeleine. She is the author of four other cookbooks. For several weeks each year, Madeleine tours the country teaching classes at cooking schools from coast to coast.